C. J. Ch...

CONQUERING

EXTREME EXPEDITIONS

THE WORLD

PUFFIN BOOKS

For William, Phoebe, Justin and Georgina

PUFFIN BOOKS

Published by the Penguin Group
Penguin Books Ltd, 27 Wrights Lane, London W8 5TZ, England
Penguin Putnam Inc., 375 Hudson Street, New York, New York 10014, USA
Penguin Books Australia Ltd, Ringwood, Victoria, Australia
Penguin Books Canada Ltd, 10 Alcorn Avenue, Toronto, Ontario, Canada M4V 3B2
Penguin Books (NZ) Ltd, Private Bag 102902, NSMC, Auckland, New Zealand

On the World Wide Web at: www.penguin.com

Penguin Books Ltd, Registered Offices: Harmondsworth, Middlesex, England

First published 2000
1 3 5 7 9 10 8 6 4 2

Text copyright © Catherine Charley, 2000
Painting by Van Everdingen, page 14, supplied by Mary Evans Picture Library
Engraving, page 25, supplied by Mary Evans Picture Library
Engraving by O. W. Brierly, page 27, supplied by Mary Evans Picture Library
Painting, page 29, supplied by Mary Evans Picture Library
Photograph, page 43, supplied by West Australia News/PPL
Photograph, page 51, supplied by Kurt Arrigo/PPL
Photograph, page 69, supplied by Chichester Archive/PPL
Photograph, page 83, supplied by The Royal Aeranautical Society
Photograph, page 93, Martyn Hayhow, supplied by PA News
Photograph, page 99, supplied by PA News
Photograph, page 109, Fiona Hanson, supplied by PA News
Photograph, page 24, © Lori Adamski Peek, supplied by Tony Stone Images

Set in Futura Book

Made and printed in England by Clays Ltd, St Ives plc

British Library Cataloguing in Publication Data
A CIP catalogue record for this book is available from the British Library

ISBN 0-141-30346-8

Contents

'I KNOW THAT I AM KNOCKING ON DEATH'S DOOR.'

There was a loud bang, and then the whole world turned upside-down. Within seconds, solo sailor Tony Bullimore had been thrown on to the ceiling of his yacht. The floor was now above him!

He was trapped under his upturned boat in the stormiest sea in the world, the freezing Southern Ocean, hundreds of miles south of Australia. It was like being thrown around in a tiny cupboard, an enclosed space that felt horribly like a coffin. Would anyone be able to rescue him?

But why was he there? What was Bullimore doing sailing alone in the middle of this vast ocean? Read on to find out about extreme explorers like him who try to conquer the world – and the dangers that they face.

ROUND-THE-WORLD ADVENTURERS TALK ABOUT THEIR EXTREME EXPEDITIONS

'In the pit of my stomach, deep down where even the butterflies are afraid to go, I know that I am knocking on death's door.'

Solo sailor Tony Bullimore, trapped under his yacht hundreds of miles off the Australian coast, January 1997

'At first, when the balloon ruptured at 8,800 m, my reaction was disappointment that I wasn't going to fly around the world. But then, as I continued my descent, I realized I was more concerned about just living.'

Balloonist Steve Fossett, after being rescued from the shark-infested Coral Sea off Australia, August 1998

'There's so much happening that you're never really frightened. That always comes afterwards, when you realize what you've gone through.'

Jeanna Yeager, co-pilot of *Voyager*, the first aircraft to fly round the world without refuelling, December 1986

'I was after adventure, plain and simple.'
Rob Penn, solicitor turned world cyclist, October 1998

'The real reason is to do something that's never been done, to be the first! To take something that seems impossible and to go ahead and do it, no matter what.'
David Kunst, the first man to walk round the world (1970–74)

'So Mr Fogg ... had made his journey around the world in 80 days. To this end he had made use of ... liners, railways, carriages, yachts, trading vessels, sledges, elephants.'
Jules Verne, Around the World in Eighty Days, 1873

'The world is 70 per cent water and built to be sailed round. It's a perfect racetrack.'
Sir Robin Knox-Johnston, the first man to sail around the world solo and non-stop, as he attempted to break another record, 1993

'All I'd like now is a change of clothes and a holiday.'
Brian Milton, after becoming the first man to fly round the globe in a microlight aircraft, July 1998

WHAT A WORLD!

The world, our Earth, is a planet that circles the Sun. Most of it is covered in water. The land areas range from the freezing ice-covered continent of Antarctica to the hot deserts of Africa.

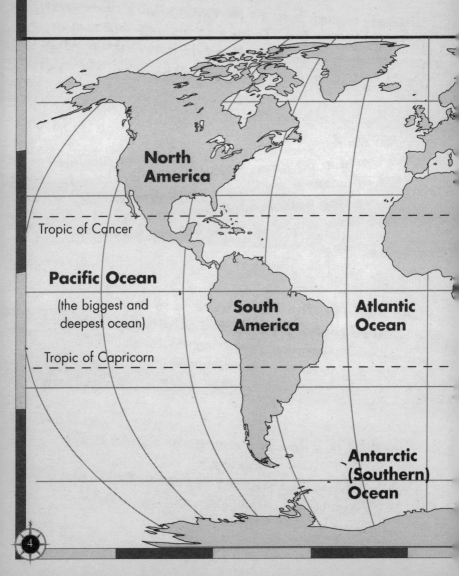

North America

Tropic of Cancer

Pacific Ocean

(the biggest and deepest ocean)

Tropic of Capricorn

South America

Atlantic Ocean

Antarctic (Southern) Ocean

There are enormously high mountains and incredibly deep oceans. Extreme explorers have all this to cope with when they travel round the world!

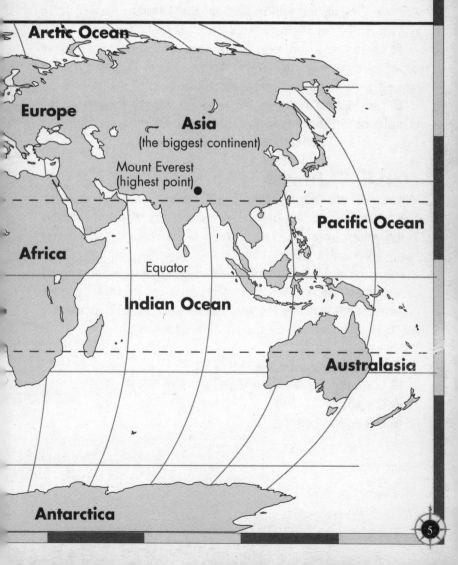

Arctic Ocean

Europe

Asia
(the biggest continent)

Mount Everest
(highest point)

Pacific Ocean

Africa

Equator

Indian Ocean

Australasia

Antarctica

WORLD FACTS

It is estimated that the total area of the Earth's surface is 510 million square km.

● There are five oceans covering 71 per cent of the surface. The largest is the Pacific Ocean, followed by the Atlantic Ocean, the Indian Ocean, the Antarctic Ocean (also known as the Southern Ocean) and the Arctic Ocean.

● There are seven main land masses, called continents. In order of size they are: Asia, Africa, North America, South America, Antarctica, Europe, Australasia.

● The highest point in the world is Mount Everest in the Himalayas – 8,848 m high. The lowest point is the Marlana Trench, in the Pacific Ocean – 11,034 m deep.

WORLD CLIMATE

When we talk about climate we mean the usual weather conditions in a certain area. There are many different climates in the world, from the freezing cold of the Poles to the burning heat of the Sahara desert.

The most important factor in deciding climate is the amount of heat from the sun which an area gets; for example, places on or near the Equator are very hot all year round because the sun is usually directly overhead. Other factors are:

● The distance from the sea
● The height of the land
● The winds
● The ocean currents

WORLD CLIMATE MAP

Polar Regions
Extremely cold and dry (has reached –89°C in Antarctica), with strong winds

Cold Regions
Cold winter (as low as –30°C) and short summer, low rainfall

Cold Temperate Regions
Warm summers but very cold winters, often below freezing

Warm Temperate Regions
Mild, wet winters and hot summers, with little rain

Tropical Regions
Very warm all year with heavy rain near equator. Also very humid

Dry Regions
Very little rain. In hot desert areas temperatures can reach more than 52°C

SOMETHING ALL EXPLORERS HAVE TO KNOW

Explorers and adventurers need to know exactly where they are when travelling the world. On their maps, lines called **latitude** and **longitude** are used. These are imaginary lines that cut up the world.

Exact measurements of latitude and longitude are made in degrees (written °) and even smaller measurements called minutes (written ´). One degree is equivalent to about 111 km and a minute to about 1.85 km.

Lines of latitude (sometimes called parallels) run round the Earth parallel to the Equator (see opposite). They are used on maps to measure distances in degrees north and south of the Equator. 1° north is just above the equator, 1° south just below it

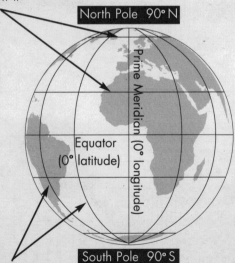

North Pole 90°N

Prime Meridian (0° longitude)

Equator (0° latitude)

South Pole 90°S

Lines of longitude (sometimes called meridians) cut up the world like segments of an orange. They give distances in degrees east or west of the prime meridian (see opposite). The Poles are found where lines of longitude meet at the top and bottom of the globe

Important lines of latitude and longitude

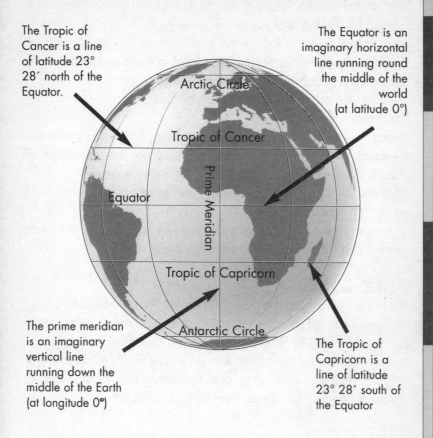

The Tropic of Cancer is a line of latitude 23° 28′ north of the Equator.

The Equator is an imaginary horizontal line running round the middle of the world (at latitude 0°)

Arctic Circle

Tropic of Cancer

Prime Meridian

Equator

Tropic of Capricorn

Antarctic Circle

The prime meridian is an imaginary vertical line running down the middle of the Earth (at longitude 0°)

The Tropic of Capricorn is a line of latitude 23° 28′ south of the Equator

The Tropics of Cancer and Capricorn mark the edge of the tropical (very hot) zone that runs round the centre of the Earth. The measurement round each of them is 22,858 miles (36,785 km). This is the distance a plane has to fly round the world to set an official record (see page 12).

The distance around the Equator is 24,855 miles (40,075 km). This is the distance a car has to cover by road to set an official world record (see page 11).

OCEAN CURRENTS

Sea water travels around the world in currents. These are formed by the force of the wind pushing on the water, which is why ocean currents follow the direction of the winds. Warm currents of water help to heat the land in their path while cold currents bring colder conditions.

WORLD WINDS

When sailors go on voyages around the world, they use the winds to help them. The main winds south of the continents of Africa, Australasia and America (i.e. in the latitudes of 30°–50°) usually blow from the west. This means it is quicker and easier for a boat to sail around the world from west to east.

In the tropical regions on either side of the equator, the main winds used by sailors are called the trade winds.

TIME ZONES

The world is divided into 24 time zones, which roughly follow the lines of longitude. In each time zone, people have their own standard time, e.g. when it is 12 noon (midday) in London, it is 7 a.m. in New York, but 4 a.m. in Los Angeles. It can get very confusing when you are travelling round the world, because you need to keep changing your watch!

WORLD MAPS

Because the world is completely round, it needs to be 'stretched out' flat if we want to see it all on a map. This is called a 'projection'. One of the most common kinds of projection is shown on pages 4 and 5.

GOING GLOBAL

To make a journey all the way round the world has long been the dream of adventurers and explorers. People have:

- sailed round the globe by boat
- flown by aeroplane
- floated on the air currents in a balloon
- walked across the land
- travelled on a motorbike
- pedalled on a bicycle
- ridden in a horse-drawn carriage …

… and have travelled in lots of other ways too.

To circumnavigate (or go round) the world is a huge achievement in itself. However, these days the aim is often to try and be the *first* at something, or the *fastest*. Newspapers often report stories of people trying to break round-the-world records or trying to set new ones by doing something in a different, and possibly more difficult, way than before.

So are there any rules about going around the world?

Yes! To get into the *Guinness Book of Records* you have to follow certain rules to make sure you complete a recognized record-breaking expedition. Often these rules are set by official organizations, e.g.:

Rules for sailing round the world

(set by the World Sailing Speed Record Council)

The yacht must:
1) Start and return at the same point
2) Cross all lines of longitude
3) Cross the Equator
4) Cover at least 21,600 nautical miles

(See page 60 for the extra rules you need to know about if you are planning to sail round the world non-stop!)

Rules for flying round the world

(set by the FAI – Fédération Aeronautique Internationale)

The minimum distance an aircraft has to be flown in order to qualify for a round-the-world flight is 22,858 miles (36,785 km). This is the same as the distance round the Tropic of Cancer or Capricorn.

Navigation

When you navigate you make your way to where you want to go, whether by sea, air or land. All global explorers, especially sailors and aircraft pilots, need to be good navigators.

In order to do this you have to work out your current position, your speed and the direction in which you are moving. In the past, explorers had various methods, including using compasses and looking at the stars. Nowadays, most extreme explorers make use of man-made satellites – structures that we have sent into space to orbit the Earth. Some of these satellites are used for communication (telephone, television, etc.), some to help forecast the weather and others are used for navigation. These send out radio signals to help people find their way, letting sailors and others know exactly where they are. They can also help to pinpoint accurately the position of someone who sends out a distress signal (see Tony Bullimore's rescue, page 60). This network of satellites round the Earth is called the Global Positioning System, known as GPS.

Around the World in 80 Days!

Ever since a French writer called Jules Verne wrote this famous book back in 1873, the story of the fictional traveller, Mr Phileas Fogg, who went around the world in 80 days, has inspired many people to try and make a similar journey. In Fogg's day, travelling by aeroplane was not an option, so he travelled in a variety of ways, ranging from merchant ships to balloons to elephants! One of the most well-known people to have made the trip recently is Michael Palin (see page 130).

JOURNEYS OF THE PAST

Nowadays there are many different ways to travel round the world. But in an age before air travel and modern communications, it was sailors who had the best chance of getting round the globe. Yet 500 years ago many people didn't even know that it was possible to go completely round the world! Most Europeans thought the world was flat, made up by land at the centre totally surrounded by water. They believed that if you sailed too far across one of the oceans you would fall off the edge!

It was a very brave sailor who sailed off on a long-distance voyage into the unknown. There were just a few inaccurate maps and *lots* of worries and fears. The dangers ranged from

Being shipwrecked has always been a danger for sailors

wild storms to being shipwrecked on a strange, empty shore, and from drowning to being attacked by pirates. Or the dangers could be on board the ship itself – you might die of illness or run out of water before the ship reached land. Some people even believed that you might end up being eaten by a horrible sea monster!

So why did the early sailors set off on these terrifying expeditions at all?

The race in the fifteenth and sixteenth centuries was not to get in to the *Guinness Book of Records*, but to discover new countries and fresh trade routes – and to make money.

But like those extreme explorers who set off to circumnavigate the world today, those who took part in the early expeditions were daring adventurers who were prepared to risk their lives to achieve something new and different.

Read on for tales of danger, bravery and adventure on the seas, lands and in the skies of the world ...

CONQUERING
EXTREME EXPEDITIONS
THE WORLD

THE CRUEL SEA

A WORLD FIRST

When you are the person who does something for the very first time, there are always unexpected problems and dangers. The very first voyage round the world certainly had plenty of these!

The myth of Magellan

The person who has been given credit for travelling round the world before anyone else, a Portuguese navigator called Ferdinand Magellan, actually didn't get the whole way himself!

Magellan met with a *very* nasty death during the voyage – read on to find out more ... Many other members of his crew also died in horrible circumstances along the way.

However, just one of the ships from Magellan's original fleet of five continued on and, under the command of Sebastian d'Elcano, returned to Spain on 6 September 1522, nearly three years after Magellan and his ships had left the country.

The very first global trip had been completed!

But, although Magellan himself only made it halfway, it was his leadership and enthusiasm that had got the voyage up and running in the first place. Many people had thought Magellan was mad when he first suggested trying to sail west to find a straight across the bottom of the 'New World', America. No one thought it was possible.

A very dangerous voyage

The ships set off with more than 250 men on board but returned with only 18. Over 230 men had died during a three-year journey. All of them had faced an enormous number of dangers to be the first to go round the world.

There had been terrible storms, devastating shipwrecks, fierce mutinies, starvation, severe illnesses, and the threat of attacks from the native peoples on the lands they visited. Would the men have joined the expedition if they had known the dangers? Well, many of the crew probably had no choice. A lot of sailors on voyages like these were press-ganged (forced) into going. Many others were criminals, desperate to leave the country before they were caught. Magellan's crew was a very mixed bunch indeed.

EXTREME FACTS
THE PERILS OF SEA VOYAGES

Storms – Magellan's small ships were badly tossed around in any storms that blew up and being wrecked was always a possibility.

Shipwreck – if the worst happened and your ship was wrecked you might manage to get on to a raft or get to the shore. But in those days, there was no radio or any other form of communication to let rescuers know where you were. You had to depend on yourself to survive. When one of Magellan's ships was wrecked it took a group of men four months to walk over snowy ground to get help.

Accidents on board – these were very common. Out of every 100 sailors who died on a sea voyage, 30 were killed by accidents, such as falling overboard or slipping from the rigging. Very little care was taken over the crew's safety in those times.

Starvation – ships often didn't carry enough food and water. The voyage might take much longer than expected and by then supplies would have run out.

Illnesses – in these cramped conditions, disease spread quickly. Some men died of diseases like malaria, which were picked up in foreign lands. Many others suffered from scurvy, a big problem for sailors at this time. No one knew what caused it but *everyone* knew about the symptoms:

- Swollen, painful joints
- Bleeding from blackened gums and scalp
- Sores breaking out all over the body … and eventual death

We now know that scurvy is caused by a lack of vitamin C, which is found in fresh fruit and vegetables. Of course, sailors in the fifteenth and sixteenth centuries couldn't get much fresh food. All of Magellan's crew suffered badly from scurvy, and many of them died from it during the voyage. Magellan was lucky enough to avoid it, maybe because he had brought his own personal supply of marmalade with him!

Pirate attack – Pirates were the highwaymen of the seas. They would cruise around the ocean looking for ships from which they could steal the cargo. As most goods were transported by sea, the rewards for pirates could be fantastic. Often ships (like Spanish treasure ships coming home from the

Americas) had valuable cargo, such as gold, on board.
Bloodthirsty and cruel, the pirates of Magellan's time didn't
care how many they killed when they attacked a ship. Sailors
often suffered horrible deaths at their hands, and many were
made to 'walk the plank'. No wonder everyone was terrified
at the thought of seeing a pirate ship looming on the horizon!

Fights – Another major cause of death was getting into
fights with native peoples, something which caused
Magellan's own death as well as many of his crew.

Preparing for the first circumnavigation

Spain and Portugal were deadly enemies in the sixteenth century. Magellan was Portuguese. So why did he set out from Spain
– an enemy country – on his epic journey? Well, unfortunately his
own king wouldn't put him in charge of an expedition, so
Magellan then asked the most powerful ruler in Europe for help,
the King of Spain.

Magellan wanted to sail an entirely new route. At this time
Europeans only knew of an eastwards route round Africa to get
to the Spice Islands. Magellan would go westwards, to try and
find a channel across the American continent (which Columbus,
another Portuguese navigator, had found in 1492 with Spanish
support). He would then see if he could reach China, India and
the Spice Islands this way.

The King of Spain saw that money could be made from
Magellan's expedition if it was successful. Magellan was made
commander of the fleet and it was agreed that he would be
allowed to keep 5 per cent of any profit the trip made.

It then took Magellan a year to get his ships and crew togeth-
er. Magellan himself was the only officer who wasn't Spanish.
The rest of the crew was made up of a mixture of nationalities –
French, Greek, North African, as well as Spanish and Portuguese.

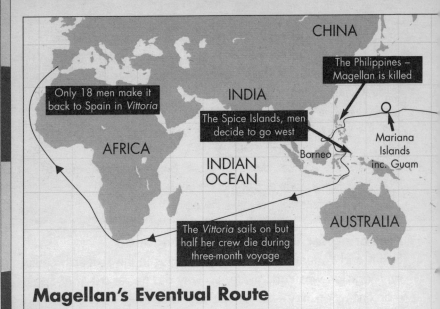

CHINA

The Philippines –
Magellan is killed

INDIA

Only 18 men make it
back to Spain in *Vittoria*

The Spice Islands, men
decide to go west

Mariana
Islands
inc. Guam

AFRICA

Borneo

INDIAN
OCEAN

The *Vittoria* sails on but
half her crew die during
three-month voyage

AUSTRALIA

Magellan's Eventual Route

Spice routes

At this time, Portugal and Spain were competing with each other on the seas, trying to find new and better trade routes to Asia. This was where goods such as silks, china and spices were bought and taken back to Europe, where they could be sold at a huge profit. Many goods were carried on land along the 'Silk Road'. They were also taken across the Indian Ocean in ships by Arabian traders.

By the beginning of the sixteenth century the Portuguese had discovered how to sail eastwards round the bottom of Africa and into the Indian Ocean. This took them to India and the Spice Islands (now called the Moluccas Islands, part of Indonesia). Discovering these routes meant that the Portuguese could bring spices to Europe in their own ships, so they no longer needed the Arab traders. Magellan and the Spanish wanted to find a western sea route.

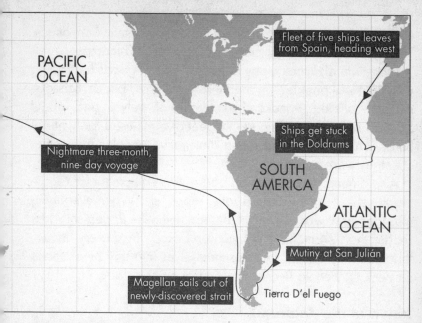

PACIFIC
OCEAN

Fleet of five ships leaves
from Spain, heading west

Nightmare three-month,
nine- day voyage

Ships get stuck
in the Doldrums

SOUTH
AMERICA

ATLANTIC
OCEAN

Mutiny at San Julián

Magellan sails out of
newly-discovered strait

Tierra D'el Fuego

Setting off

On 20 September 1519, a fleet of five ships sailed from Spain:

The *San Antonio*
The *Trinidad*
The *Concepción*
The *Santiago*
The *Vittoria*

The crew had no idea that only one ship would ever return. In fact, there were a few other things that the men didn't know about – such as, exactly where they were going. Magellan kept his plans quiet. He decided not to tell the men that they were voyaging to completely unknown territory.

The five little ships were not just packed with people but also with supplies of all kinds. As well as food for the voyage they also took a large number of weapons to protect them from attack. These included cannons, crossbows, spears and lances.

Magellan also took many different types of goods for trading with the local people. Among these were glass beads, scissors, mirrors, printed handkerchiefs, rolls of velvet and about 20,000 bells for attaching to the feet of birds used for hunting! European explorers had found that native peoples from other countries were amazed by these.

Also among the supplies on board was equipment for repairing the ships, such as spare sails, ropes, etc. When everything was loaded, it was all pretty cramped. Even the largest ship was shorter than 24 m. With 50 men on board, it was very uncomfortable. They had to squeeze themselves into any bit of space on deck they could find to sleep on at night.

Down in the doldrums

After visiting the Spanish Canary Islands, the ships sailed west across the Atlantic towards America, using the winds and currents they knew well. But then they hit the doldrums. They were stuck for two weeks with no wind to move them on or to keep them cool. The men got very bored and restless. Magellan already had a lot of enemies in the fleet. Being stuck for so long didn't help their mood.

The dismal doldrums

The doldrums are a region just north of the Equator where the winds are very light, and can be even non-existent. This is because the area lies between the different trade winds of the world (see page 10). Sailing ships often got stuck here. Sailors got depressed because they weren't getting anywhere. Hence the expression 'to be in the doldrums' – to be down in the dumps, low spirited! Even today sailing boats still get stuck in this area.

Eventually the ships escaped the boredom of the doldrums and sailed on towards Brazil. After picking up some fresh supplies at what is now Rio de Janeiro, Magellan sailed quickly on south down the coast of South America. He didn't want to hang around because the sea off Brazil was controlled by the Portuguese and Magellan was leading a Spanish-sponsored expedition. Rio de Janeiro was the last accurately recorded place on the maps that Magellan had. From now on their voyage was almost completely into the unknown.

Secret maps

When sailors returned from their expeditions they would be ordered to report any new discoveries to a central office in their own countries. The maps would then be altered to include these details. This information was top secret and was carefully kept from the hands of their enemies. They didn't want other countries finding out their trade-route secrets or getting their hands on useful – and often life-saving – information about winds, currents, tides and newly found areas of land.

Mutiny!

Magellan decided to winter the ships in the rocky and barren bay of San Julián, in southern Argentina. It was a terrible stormy winter and food supplies were short.

Resentment against Magellan grew among the crew. The other officers hated him, especially as he wasn't Spanish. By now they had caught on to Magellan's plans to search for the unknown passage. Nearly everyone thought that he was mad to try and sail so far south.

On 1 April 1520, the captains of the *Concepción*, *San Antonio* and *Vittoria* came to tell Magellan that they wished to be consulted in future about the fleet's course and that their crews did not want to sail any further down the South American coast. Magellan sent them back to their ships.

That night a group of mutineers tried to take control of three ships, but Magellan showed the leadership, determination – and ruthlessness – that was needed to crush them. After a short but nasty struggle, he regained control of the whole fleet. Magellan then ordered the captain of the *Vittoria* to be killed and his body hanged from the rigging.

The next morning Magellan had this body quartered (chopped up into pieces). These were displayed on all the ships as a warning to the rest of the men. Next he made the crews watch as he commanded a servant to behead the captain of the *Concepción*. Finally, he announced that two other ringleaders would be left behind when the expedition sailed off. They were never heard of again.

Forty other mutineers were sentenced to death. However, Magellan knew it would be foolish to get rid of so many of his crew because he would need them for the long journey ahead. He changed their sentences to hard labour for the rest of the time they were in the bay. The men were clapped in irons.

Magellan had wanted to frighten his crew and, for the time being, his tactics seemed to work.

EXTREME FACTS
MUTINIES

A mutiny is an uprising by soldiers or sailors against their superiors. Mutinies happened quite often on ships in Magellan's time because the conditions were so terrible.

One of the most famous ship mutinies ever was on HMS *Bounty* in the Pacific ocean in 1789. Captain Bligh was so hard and strict that the crew decided to get rid of him. They mutinied and set him adrift in an open boat, along with 18 other men. Incredibly, this boat reached safety 4,000 miles (6,500 km) later! The mutineers sailed on in the *Bounty* until they reached Pitcairn Island, in the Pacific Ocean. They were not discovered until 1808 – nearly 20 years later!

Mutiny was a very serious offence. This drawing shows the kind of punishment a mutinous sailor could expect!

Shipwreck!

Having regained control of his men, Magellan continued on his way. The stormy weather, however, caused a tragedy: the *Santiago* was wrecked while exploring further down the coast. Some of its crew had to make a terrible four-month overland journey back to the other ships before the remaining crew and cargo could be rescued. This did not improve the mood of the men.

Success ... and problems

Eventually, on 21 October 1520, an entrance to a possible channel, or strait, was spotted, between high cliffs. Was this it? Magellan sent two ships to check. Five days later they returned, announcing that the channel widened further on! Magellan was very excited. He felt that this was the route he had been searching for. But others were less enthusiastic. As they sailed along the channel they saw rows of corpses stuck on poles. It seemed that this was not a place where friendly people lived.

Although the men couldn't see anyone on shore, at night the sky was lit by the glow of thousands of distant fires that the native peoples had lit. Magellan gave the area the name Tierra del Fuego, 'Land of Fire', which is what it is still called. It was very spooky. Some of the men became very frightened about the dangers that were perhaps waiting for them further along the channel. Their fears grew until ... the crew of the *San Antonio*, the largest ship in the fleet, mutinied. They over-powered their captain and, with relief, set off back to Spain.

Discovering the Magellan Strait

With one wrecked and another making its way home, Magellan only had three ships left. But he continued on, exploring this channel, which proved to be narrow, winding, dangerous and stormy, with a strong wind. At times the wind against them was so fierce that they had to tow the ships with rowing boats. They sailed past rough, rocky ground and snow-capped mountains, often checking new inlets in case they might be the way out of the channel. No one knew if there definitely *was* a way out. It was only Magellan's determination and discipline that kept them going.

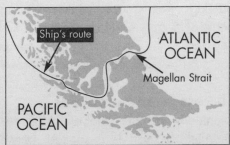

Ship's route

ATLANTIC OCEAN

Magellan Strait

PACIFIC OCEAN

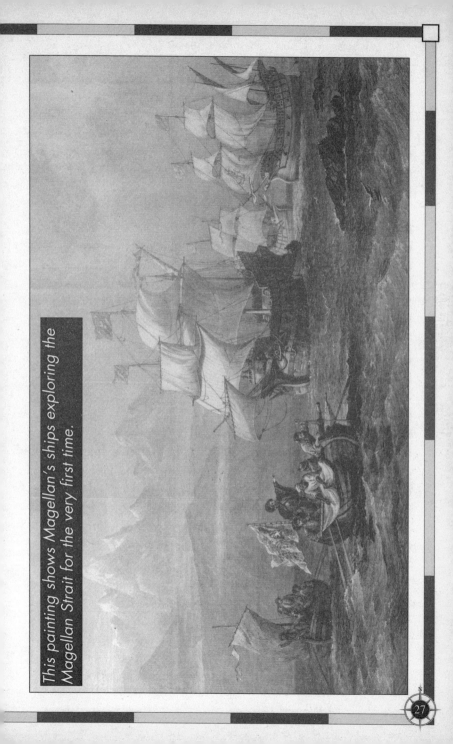

This painting shows Magellan's ships exploring the Magellan Strait for the very first time.

But he was proved right! After 38 days and 334 miles (540 km) the three little ships sailed out into flat, open water. Magellan called this the 'Sea of Peace', or the Pacific Ocean, because it was so calm in contrast to the violent waters of the channel. He had changed the course of history by charting a route that linked the Atlantic and Pacific Oceans. The strait now bears his name.

A worse nightmare

But the troubles of Magellan's men were not over yet. In fact, things were to get worse, much worse ...

Magellan believed that it was now just a short distance to the Spice Islands – only a matter of a few days. He had no idea that the ships had just entered the biggest stretch of water in the world. It was to be a terrible three months and nine days in the vast emptiness of the Pacific Ocean before the ships touched land.

Starvation

Food began to run out, fresh water became scarce. Men died from scurvy or starvation or collapsed from total exhaustion and despair. It was a dreadful time. Those who found themselves still alive were driven to eating rats, sawdust and boiled-up pieces of leather. They drank stagnant, foul, smelly water in their desperation. They did not know if this horrendous journey would ever end. Perhaps the tales of falling off the end of the world were true after all, some of them thought.

Ships' food

Ships setting out on long voyages had to carry a lot of food and water. But supplies were limited by space and by how long the food could last. Main provisions on ships of Magellan's time would have included:

- Rice
- Flour (to make bread)
- Salted meat and fish (salted to preserve it)
- Oil and vinegar
- Water in oak barrels (which could become contaminated)
- Wine or beer
- Ship's biscuit (a large part of the sailors' diet, often full of beetles, sometimes mouldy, and also liked by starving rats!)
- Dried peas and lentils

At the beginning of the voyage the sailors would have had some fresh vegetables and perhaps some live animals (like chickens and pigs). But neither of these would have lasted for long. Nowadays, modern sailors take supplies of tinned or freeze-dried food and usually have refrigerators on board. There is also no need to carry water as many boats have desalinators, equipment which turns sea water into fresh water.

On Magellan's voyage, food became so short that if a crew member was lucky enough to catch one of the ship's rats, it could be sold as a meal for half a ducat (a gold coin)!

'Land ahoy!'
On 6 March 1521 the island of Guam was sighted. It was an

incredible relief when the ships were able to anchor and send par-
ties ashore to find fresh food and water. But the months of isola-
tion made the men nervous of the native peoples who came
out to them in canoes with fruits and coconuts to trade.
Misunderstandings arose and Magellan ordered the shooting of
some of the islanders and burned their village to set an example.

Hacked to death

The ships sailed on to the Philippines, where Magellan put sick sailors
ashore to recover from the voyage and traded with the local people.
One local chief became a good friend and he asked Magellan to
attack his enemies on another island. The battle was brief and
Magellan was hit with a poison-tipped spear and then hacked to
death. Eight of his men were also killed. It was 27 April 1521.

What now?

The terrors for the remaining members of Magellan's crew in the
Philippines continued. The two captains who now took command
proved as bad as Magellan at dealing with the people of the
islands. At a banquet hosted by a local leader they too were
killed, together with 25 of their sailors.

Let's get out of here!

It seemed a very good idea to leave the Philippines, which the
ships duly did. But all three were now in very bad shape after two
years of wild seas, in particular the *Concepción*. Her wooden hull
was being eaten away by worms and she had begun to sink. It
was decided that she should be stripped, abandoned and
burned, and her crew transferred to the other two ships. In all,
there were now only 115 sailors.

The Spice Islands – at last!

After more adventures – including dining off plates of gold in the palace of the rich Muslim ruler of Brunei and escaping from a trap he had set to capture their ships – the sailors finally reached the place that had been the aim of the whole expedition, the Spice Islands, in November 1521.

The two ships were filled up with cloves, cinnamon, nutmegs, mace and sandalwood – bought at a good price. Everyone was much happier than they had been for a long time. If they could just get back to Spain they would be rich!

A diary of the voyage

We know about all the details of Magellan's voyage because of the diaries of an Italian nobleman, Antonio Pigafetta. Pigafetta had sailed from Spain with Magellan's fleet and was one of the 18 men who finally returned to Spain in the *Vittoria*. Two years later he published his diaries. He wrote about everything on the voyage - from the mutinies to the bad water, from the lack of food to the man-eating sharks.

He described how 'great fish' (sharks) approached their ships. The men had never seen creatures like this before:

'They have terrible teeth and eat men when they find them alive or dead in the sea.'

He also wrote about the nightmare three-month long voyage across the Pacific, saying how:

'... we ate only old biscuit turned to powder, all full of worms and stinking of the urine which the rats had made on it, having eaten the good. And we drank water impure and yellow.'

Yet more dangers

But the dangers were not yet over for these men, and they knew it. They now had to choose which way they went home to Europe – eastwards or westwards. Going west meant sailing through waters which were dominated by their enemies, the Portuguese. However, going east meant returning the same way they had come. The idea of repeating the same journey (and maybe facing again the horrors of the last two years) was too much for them. They decided to continue westwards across the Indian Ocean and risk running into their enemies. This was a crucial decision. Without intending to they had decided to sail completely around the world!

Only one ship left ...
But just before they set off the *Trinidad* was discovered to be leaking. It was decided that the *Vittoria* would set off for Spain on her own, to catch the favourable winds. Under the command of Captain Sebastián d'Elcano, she sailed out into the Indian Ocean, trying to avoid the Portuguese trading routes as much as possible. She went round the Cape of Good Hope at the bottom of Africa. She was lucky in that she didn't come across any Portuguese, but the conditions on the long journey were nearly as bad as the voyage across the Pacific.

More deaths
Again, men began to die of scurvy and faced starvation. In three months they only landed once, and this was on an uninhabited island. The seas were rough and the ship was leaking badly. Captain d'Elcano faced mutiny. By the time the *Vittoria* entered the Atlantic only half the crew who had set off from the Spice Islands were still alive. The bodies of their dead companions had been given to the sea.

As the damaged *Vittoria* limped towards Spain, the crew begged the captain to throw some of the spices overboard to make the ship lighter. But d'Elcano refused. He knew that the Spanish king and the merchants who had financed the expedition would not take kindly to hearing that the valuable cargo had been thrown into the sea.

Heroes!

The *Vittoria* staggered on and returned to her home port of Seville in Spain on 8 September 1522. Eighteen men set foot on Spanish soil again. They thanked God that they were still alive after all the horrors of the three-year journey. People were amazed when they heard that these men had been right the way round the world. Most hadn't thought it possible! They hadn't believed the world was round. Now it had been proved!

Captain d'Elcano was regarded as a hero. Magellan was forgotten.

But Magellan's theory had been proved: there *was* a western route to Asia from Europe. And it had been Magellan's determination to prove this that had inspired the first circumnavigation of the world.

And what of the *Trinidad*? Well, she eventually left the Spice Islands and sailed east, back across the Pacific. The crew suffered another horrific three-month voyage and were forced to turn back to the Spice Islands, where they were captured by the Portuguese. Only four of them got back to Spain, in 1525. They too had gone round the world – eventually!

DARE-DEVIL DRAKE

Sir Francis Drake, an Englishman, was the second person to lead an expedition round the world – but this was not until 60 years after Magellan's voyage.

However, Drake was the first person to set out with the *aim* of going round the world and succeeding.

In December 1577 Drake left Plymouth, England, with five ships and a crew of 164. Like Magellan's fleet, only one, the *Golden Hind*, was to complete the voyage and return to England three years later, on 26 September 1580.

Looking for plunder

Drake's mission, from Queen Elizabeth I, was:

1 To take possession of any territory he could find south of the Magellan Strait. It was believed that here was the top of another large continent, Terra Australis. However, he discovered that Tierra del Fuego was probably just an island and not the edge of a continent.

2 'Unofficially' to attack Spanish treasure ships and ports on the unprotected west coast of South America.

EXTREME FACTS
PRIVATEERS

Privateers were another peril for sailors at this time. Like pirates, they attacked rich cargo ships and stole from them. However, unlike pirates, privateers were 'unofficially' sponsored by their governments

Sir Francis Drake has been called a privateer. He managed to capture a lot of Spanish ships and their treasure – gold, silver and precious gems from South America. Queen Elizabeth I herself made £300,000 from Drake's voyage, an *enormous* sum of money then. It's no wonder that, a year after his return, Queen Elizabeth knighted Drake on his ship the *Golden Hind*.

But Drake's voyage was not all 'plain sailing'. Like Magellan, and other extreme explorers on the seas in the sixteenth century, Drake and his crew suffered from scurvy, starvation, sickness, storms and attacks. There were also mutinies. But, like Magellan, Drake was tough and kept going – that is the one of the marks of an extreme explorer.

Other early circumnavigators
There were several other important circumnavigators following Drake, you can find them in the timeline on page 134.

SAILING ADVENTURES

Many great adventures have been experienced at sea since the dangerous and epic journeys of the earliest circumnavigators. At the end of the nineteenth century, some people began to consider sailing round the world just for the sake of it. One of them decided to face the challenge on his own, sailing solo.

GOING IT ALONE

The first solo circumnavigation of the world was completed in 1898 by a 54-year-old American, Captain Joshua Slocum. He was very lucky that he didn't fall overboard during his three-year trip, because he couldn't swim!

Slocum left Rhode Island on the east coast of America on 24 April 1895 and returned on 3 July 1898. Altogether he had sailed 46,000 miles (74,000 km) – all on his own.

Slocum's boat was called the *Spray* and was old-fashioned even for the late 1890s. It was a single-masted yacht, 11 m long by 4m wide. He had spent 13 months rebuilding it from a totally dilapidated state. Her top speed was 9 knots. During his voyage, in 1897, he managed to achieve a single-handed sailing record that held for 70 years – sailing 1,200 nautical miles in 8 days.

> ### Speed and distance at sea
> A knot is a unit of speed used by ships and by aircraft. A nautical mile is used for measuring distances at sea and is not the same as a mile measured on land. One nautical mile is equivalent to 1.185 km or 1.15 ordinary miles (known as statute miles). One knot per hour is equivalent to travelling at one nautical mile per hour.

Round the world

As Slocum had intended to sail round the world eastwards, he went from America across the Atlantic to Gibraltar, planning to go through the Suez Canal. But at Gibraltar he was warned about pirate attacks and so decided to sail back across the Atlantic to Brazil and down the coast of South America. He was now going westwards, like Magellan.

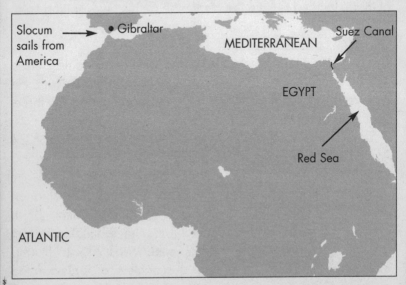

Slocum sails from America → • Gibraltar

MEDITERRANEAN

Suez Canal

EGYPT

Red Sea

ATLANTIC

Canal links

The Suez and Panama Canals are both waterways that were built to make it easier for ships to travel the world.

The Suez Canal links the Mediterranean and the Red Sea so that ships travelling from Europe to Asia don't need to sail round the Cape of Good Hope. It was completed in 1869 and is 100 miles (162 km) long.

The Panama Canal in Central America connects the Atlantic and Pacific Oceans so ships don't have to go all the way round Cape Horn. It was opened in 1914 and is 50 miles (82 km) in length.

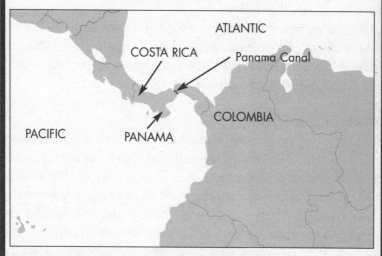

Stormy weather

Off southern Argentina, Slocum got caught in a wild storm and at one stage was nearly sunk by an enormous wave. He describes this terrifying event in his book, *Sailing Alone Around the World*:

A tremendous wave, the culmination, it seemed, of many waves, rolled down on her [the Spray] ... roaring as it came ... I saw the mighty crest towering masthead-high above me. The mountain of water submerged my vessel. She shook in every timber and reeled under the great weight of the sea ... it may have been a minute that from my hold in the rigging I could see no part of the Spray's hull.

Slocum's life flashed before him; he thought this was the end. But luckily, the *Spray* 'rose quickly out of it, and rolled grandly over the rollers that followed.'

The *Spray* managed to get through the terrible storm, but she was badly damaged and needed lots of repairs. In fact (like all sailors) Slocum spent a great deal of time on his journey repairing damaged sails and broken equipment.

Stuck in the Strait

Slocum sailed on into the Magellan Strait, where he had more bad weather. The winds against him were so strong as he reached the end of the strait that it was only on his seventh attempt that he actually managed to sail out into the Pacific!

As Magellan had found when he entered the Pacific, the weather was much better. Slocum now intended to sail around the bottom of Australia, and so arrived in Melbourne. Here he made himself a bit of extra money by catching a 3.5-m shark and charging the locals sixpence each for a look. In this way he was able to pay the port charges – and have a bit left over!

After Melbourne Slocum came across icebergs and bad weather in the Southern Ocean and he decided to go round the north coast of Australia instead.

Next he crossed the Indian Ocean, sailing with the trade winds. This is where he set his speed record of 1,200 miles in 8 days. In November 1897 he got to South Africa, where he spent four months. Eventually he set off again and, after rounding the Cape of Good Hope, he set off up the Atlantic.

Hurricane horror

The weather on his homeward journey turned out to be some of the worst he had faced on the whole voyage. First of all he had no wind for a whole week (always bad for a sailor), then he had the very opposite problem. The *Spray* was hit by a series of wild gales. The winds were so fierce that bits broke off the mast. Slocum fixed up his boat as best he could as the gales battered him for days and nights. Exhausted, he tried to keep on course.

Finally he approached the coast near New York, not far from Rhode Island – and home! But, just as he was hoping for calmer seas, he hit a hurricane that had just caused havoc in New York itself. He now had to face not only wild, screaming winds, but hard hail and fierce electrical thunderstorms. All he could do was tie everything down, take in the sails and put down the sea anchor (usually a canvas bag that fills with water and slows the yacht down). Then he went and lay on his bunk as the storms tossed his little yacht around mercilessly. There was not much else he could do, except to hope that the *Spray* and he would survive this terrifying ordeal.

And they did! After the hurricane had passed he was still alive. The weather became kinder to him and he sailed on to a great reception on Rhode Island, from where he had set out over three years earlier.

A variety of welcomes

At most places where Slocum landed during his trip he was greeted with great excitement because people had heard of this

American sailing alone round the world. Often he did not have to pay any fees for anchoring in harbours. He was quite a celebrity. But sometimes people were not so welcoming. When he was sailing through Magellan Strait he sprinkled the deck of the *Spray* with carpet tacks at night to provide him with a warning system in case any of the local people tried to attack him while he slept. And it worked! One night he was woken up by loud screams and shouts as the tacks pierced the invaders' bare feet!

Ghostly company?

Early in the voyage Slocum had passed out in pain on the cabin floor, suffering from a severe stomach-ache. When he came round he realized the *Spray* was caught in a terrible gale and he rushed up on deck in a panic. As he came up from the cabin, he stopped in amazement when he saw a strange figure standing at the wheel. He looked like a pirate – a tall, weather-beaten sailor with shaggy, black whiskers, wearing a large red cap! How had a wild-looking stranger suddenly appeared on his yacht in the middle of the ocean? Slocum was terrified. Afterwards, he wrote:

While I gazed upon his threatening aspect I forgot the storm, and wondered if he had come to cut my throat. 'Señor,' said he, doffing his cap, 'I have come to do you no harm.' And a smile, the faintest in the world, but still a smile, played on his face, which seemed not unkind when he spoke ... 'I am one of Columbus's crew,' he continued, 'I am the pilot of the Pinta come to aid you. Lie quiet, señor captain,' he added, 'and I will guide your ship tonight ...

Columbus's ship, the *Pinta*, had sailed to America in 1492, more than 400 years earlier!

The following day, when Slocum had recovered and was able to sail the yacht again himself, he found, to his amazement, that the *Spray* had continued steadily on her course, with a good speed, through the night. The ghostly sailor had done his job well.

The ghost appeared to Slocum in a dream the next time he slept saying he would look after him during the voyage. He spoke to him politely, raised his cap and disappeared as mysteriously as he had come!

It had been a weird experience, but Slocum definitely felt that he had been helped through the storm by this spectral sailor from times past.

EXTREME FACTS
GHOSTS AT SEA

Slocum is not the only lone sailor with a ghostly tale. Solo yachtswoman Ann Davison tells how, at the end of an exhausting sail across the Atlantic in the 1950's, all she wanted to do was go to sleep. But she couldn't. In fact she needed to be at her most alert because of all the other ships in the busy waters.

Yet, as in a dream, she became aware that there were two other people on deck with her. One quietly sitting and the other checking the sails. Who were they? Where had they come from? She had no idea. But she was so tired it didn't seem odd when they told her to go and lie down, while they kept watch. She meekly did what they said, leaving her yacht in their hands. When she awoke the following morning she went up to thank them. The yacht was sailing safely, but they had completley disappeared ...

In fact, there are many tales told by solo sailors, mountaineers and other extreme explorers of feeling that there is someone with them when the going gets really tough. Is it all imagination, or is there really a ghostly presence helping them?

ALONE ... AND FAST

In the first half of the twentieth century, especially in between the two world wars, many yachts of various sizes were sailed round the world. Most of their skippers were not really trying to break records but took their time, enjoying the sailing trip of a lifetime.

That is until the 1960s, when an Englishman, Francis Chichester, decided he was going to sail round the world, not just alone, but as fast as he could, with only one stop on the way. Why?

Five years earlier he had been told he had serious lung cancer. Chichester was determined to fight it and after two years of treatment he was told he was in the clear. However, the doctors said that he would have to be careful for the rest of his life.

Chichester had always been a rebel and this advice made him want to try to do as many exciting things as possible in the time he had left. Twice he sailed alone across the Atlantic. But this wasn't enough of a challenge for him. He was 62 when he decided on his world trip. By the time he set off he was nearly 65, an age when most men are retiring and putting their feet up!

Chichester was going to spend longer at sea alone than anyone else had ever done. He planned to go eastwards in a brand-new yacht designed specially for the journey, *Gipsy Moth IV*. He left England on 27 August 1966.

Sailing eastwards

Most people sailing round the world nowadays go eastwards. It is quicker and easier because the main winds and currents in the Southern Ocean move in this direction.

Frances Chichester sails solo on the Gipsy Moth.

Chichester had timed each of his two journey legs to be about 100 days. The most important aims were to keep himself fit and the yacht in good condition. He tried to eat well and he practised yoga. But, alone in a small space, you may find that even little things annoy you more than usual. Among other things, Chichester was driven mad by the sounds of tins continuously rattling in their store!

EXTREME FACTS
COPING ALONE AT SEA

Loneliness is one of the greatest problems for a solo long-distance sailor. Some people can cope with being on their own for a long time and some people can't. The solo sailor has to make *all* the decisions alone, has to sort out *all* problems alone, has to do *everything* alone.

Boredom is also a big problem when the wind is weak and the yacht is stuck in a place such as the doldrums. There is no one to help pass the time. Sailors try to keep themselves busy by doing work on their yachts, such as repairing sails. At least when things get tough or dangerous there is no time to get bored, but that is another occasion when it would be extremely useful to have another person for advice, practical help and to keep your spirits up.

Most solo sailors have radios for communication on their yachts, but that is not the same as having someone with you on the trip. Could *you* spend months totally on your own with just a radio as your only contact with other people?

Celebrations

Like most solo sailors, Chichester tried to keep his spirits up by creating special events. For example, on his 65th birthday he dressed smartly and drank champagne. Other solo sailors have brightened themselves up in a similar way. Goss (see page 73) had special food packages for celebration days like his birthday and Christmas Day. Others make an event out of everything, even something like cutting their hair!

Chichester sailed round Cape Horn into an area known as the Roaring Forties. Here seas were different from any he had sailed in before – enormous, powerful and frightening. It was very tough, especially when his self-steering equipment broke. This is standard equipment for a modern-day sailor. It holds the yacht on a pre-set course and so allows the solo yachtsman to eat, sleep or to do other necessary jobs.

> ## The Roaring Forties and Fifties
> The Roaring Forties is the name given by sailors to the treacherous seas at 40° latitude south – the fierce waters of the Southern Ocean. They are well known for being very rough, with gale-force winds. The seas at 50° latitude south, the Roaring Fifties, are even worse!

Fighting spirit

Without the self-steering, Chichester thought he wouldn't be able to reach Sydney, and complete the first part of his journey, in 100 days. He became very depressed and didn't feel he could continue. But after a while he pulled himself together and used his initiative – what every extreme explorer needs to succeed! He eventually managed to set up a simple self-steering system that worked if the wind wasn't too strong, and he made good progress with it. He reached Sydney after 107 days at sea – very good going in the circumstances.

He looked terrible – covered in cuts and bruises and much thinner, having lost 19 kg in weight. People tried to persuade him to give up his quest. But Chichester was determined to sail on. However, just 36 hours after he left Sydney, *Gipsy Moth* capsized in heavy seas and was very badly damaged. Chichester could only sail on slowly now as he repaired her. He wrote at this time:

'I could not be more depressed. Everything seems wrong with this voyage. I hate it and am frightened.'

Yet he kept himself going. He sailed on round Cape Horn and into the Atlantic. The lack of progress he made in the doldrums – so near now to his home port – made him very homesick.

But on 28 May 1967 he made it! He sailed into Plymouth harbour 9 months and 7 days after he had left. He was a hero! Thousands of people came to cheer him. The media was there to greet him too.

On 7 July 1967 Queen Elizabeth II knighted him in Plymouth. Like an earlier Sir Francis (see page 33), Chichester was an Englishman who had conquered the seas of the world!

THE GOLDEN GLOBE RACE

So who was going to be the first to sail round the world alone *without* touching land?

That was the question on many people's lips after Sir Francis Chichester's adventure. Several sailors began to think about attempting this challenge.

Soon the media began to get interested and then *The Sunday Times* newspaper, which had been Chichester's main sponsor, turned the idea into a competition called the Golden Globe Race. The Golden Globe was the trophy on offer for the first person round the world, and there was also a cash prize of £5,000 for the fastest time.

The Sunday Times made the entry regulations as few, and as simple, as possible:

• Start date: between 1 June and 31 October 1968. This was to try and avoid the worst weather conditions in the Southern Ocean.

• A yacht's departure and return should be recorded by a national newspaper or magazine.

• Yachts could set out from any port in the British Isles and return to it, after having sailed round the three great capes of the Southern Ocean: Cape of Good Hope (South Africa), Cape Leeuwin (Western Australia) and Cape Horn (South America).

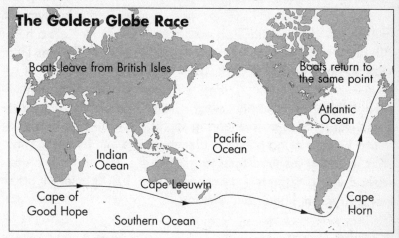

The Golden Globe Race

Boats leave from British Isles

Boats return to the same point

Atlantic Ocean

Pacific Ocean

Indian Ocean

Cape of Good Hope

Cape Leeuwin

Cape Horn

Southern Ocean

Automatic entries

The rules meant that those who were already preparing to attempt a non-stop, round-the-world, solo record would automatically be included in *The Sunday Times'* race, whether they liked it or not.

Nine people set out. Of these, five had to give up before they left the Atlantic. The adventures and disasters that befell the four men left in the race – Tetley, Crowhurst, Moitessier and Knox-Johnston – were to provide much greater excitement and more anguish than anyone had ever imagined.

Golden Globe adventures

Nigel Tetley was in the lead in *Victress*. He had sailed down the Atlantic, rounded the three Capes and was on his way back up the Atlantic to return to his starting point of Plymouth. Suddenly a bit of news over the radio gave him a shock: *Teigmouth Electron* was coming up close behind him. Her

47

skipper, Donald Crowhurst, had been out of radio contact for months and no one had known where he was. It seemed that he had made incredibly good time and was now chasing Tetley.

Shipwreck!
After nearly 200 days of solo-sailing Tetley was determined he was going to win. Although he knew that *Victress* was in a fragile state after her long rough voyage, he pushed her as fast as possible. Then disaster struck. Tetley was asleep when he was awoken by a terrible tearing sound. He rushed up on deck to see *Victress* being pulled to pieces around him by the stormy seas. He only *just* had time to get into his life-raft before she sank. It was a tragedy: he had only been 1,000 miles (1,600 km) away from home, and victory!

A guilty secret
So did Donald Crowhurst win the race? Well ...

Just two weeks out from England, Crowhurst had realized that there was no way he could go all round the world in the *Teignmouth Electron*. He hadn't prepared properly for the voyage and there were a lot of problems with the yacht. But he didn't dare admit this over the radio to his supporters and sponsors. So he sailed on, pretending to them that everything was fine. He began to lie about his position and progress. Next, he stopped sending radio messages.

Three and a half months later, Crowhurst radioed out to the world again. He said that he had crossed the Southern Ocean and now was approaching Cape Horn from the west. This was untrue. In fact, he had never left the Atlantic Ocean. He had just sailed round and round, trying to avoid the busy shipping routes!

The sinking of the *Victress* was very bad news for Crowhurst. He didn't want to win the race: he had intended to come second. He had been writing a false log of his journey and he thought it would be examined too closely if he came first. The more Crowhurst thought about it, the more worried he got, but he couldn't avoid 'winning' the race now. Over the radio he heard that a big reception was being planned for his return.

It was all too much for him. On 1 July 1969 Crowhurst decided that it would be better if he never went back home and he slipped overboard to drown himself. It was a tragic end. Ten days later his empty yacht was found, together with his false log – and his real one.

Log
The log is a daily record that sailors make of their voyages. It includes details of position, speed, weather, technical problems and events, such as the sightings of sharks. Aircrews also keep logs of their flights.

Sea rebel

Bernard Moitessier from France was a very different type of man from Crowhurst. He had spent most of his life sailing, and was a bit of a 'sea-gypsy'! He called his yacht *Joshua* after his hero, Captain Slocum.

Moitessier was very happy at sea. In fact, he so enjoyed being alone on the oceans of the world that, as he entered the Atlantic on his way home, he decided that he didn't want to return to civilization or to win a stupid race!

So he didn't sail north towards Europe but headed on around the globe again. The world was shocked! They tried to contact him. They tried to make him think of the glory he would bring to his country. But Moitessier just wanted to be alone with the sea. He eventually stopped in Tahiti ...

In fact Moitessier was the first person to sail non-stop, solo round the world, because he crossed his outward journey line.

But, because he didn't return to his starting point, he didn't win the Golden Globe – nor does he fit the *Guinness Book of Records'* rules (see page 12).

The final hope

Robin Knox-Johnston was the only contender left for the Golden Globe. Would he make it?

Just 16 days out from England, he noticed that his yacht, *Suhaili*, was taking in water. He passed the Cape Verde Islands (off north Africa) and then put on snorkel and flippers and went overboard to see what was wrong. It was bad news. There was a great crack where the keel was joined on to the hull.

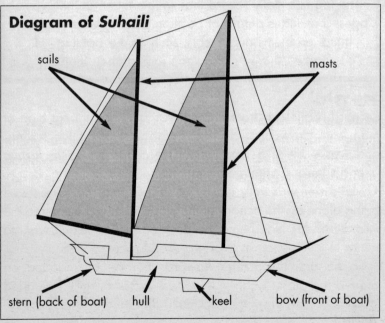

Diagram of *Suhaili*

sails

masts

stern (back of boat)   hull   keel   bow (front of boat)

The crack was about 2.5 m long and it opened and closed as the yacht rolled in the water. This would prove fatal in the treacherous seas of the Southern Ocean. He had either to give up the race or to do something about it.

For Knox-Johnston the choice was simple: he would try to block up the gap rather than give up. However, this is something that would usually be done with the yacht out of water, on dry land! Knox-Johnston was going to have to carry out the repair nearly 2 m underwater, without scuba equipment, on his own – and in a shark-infested sea!

It would be tough. The gap needed to be firmly patched up with canvas and cotton, held in place by nails. Knox-Johnston attached a hammer on a line over the side of the yacht, put on a blue shirt and jeans (to hide the whiteness of his body in an attempt to keep off the sharks), strapped a knife to his leg, and dived overboard.

The job was very difficult because he couldn't hold his breath long enough to complete the hammering. He kept trying and eventually, after several attempts, he was doing well.

Shark!

He was having a coffee break back on board when he saw a dark shape in the water. It was a shark, circling the yacht! Knox-Johnston waited. Should he shoot it? If he did, the blood and its death thrashings could bring other sharks to the area.

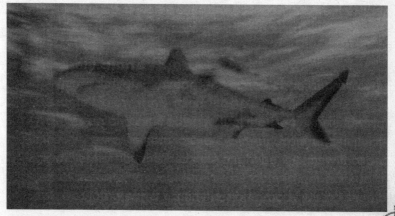

However, after ten minutes the shark was still circling and showed no sign of leaving. Knox-Johnston decided he had to get rid of it. He threw some sheets of toilet roll overboard and waited for the shark to come and have a look at these strange objects floating on the water. The shark swam up to them. Knox-Johnston fired his gun. The shark thrashed around for about half a minute, then lay still in the water. Gradually the dead creature began to sink down into the depths of the sea.

Knox-Johnston waited and watched carefully to see if any other sharks might turn up. Half an hour later he decided to go back to work on *Suhaili*. He stayed in the sea for another hour and a half, always glancing over his shoulder, looking out for other sharks. Luckily, no more turned up, but it was a very frightening experience. Two days later he completed the repair. He was a brave man.

EXTREME FACTS SHARK ATTACK!

Sharks do occasionally attack people but they probably don't go out of their way to find humans. It is quite possible that they mistake us for dolphins or other sea creatures. In fact, it seems that sharks might not really like human flesh, because it is unusual for a shark to swallow much. On the rare occasions that swimmers are attacked, it is usually with a bite to the legs. A person may die from shock and loss of blood, or drown before they are rescued.

Stories of shark attacks usually involve swimmers in very warm seas near beaches. But sharks also attack in the middle of the deep ocean. Shipwrecked sailors should try and stay on the remains of their yacht, unless of course it has totally sunk. Not only does this mean that rescuers will spot you more easily, it also means that you have more protection between yourself and a shark. Don't dangle your limbs over the side as this could attract the attention of a lurking shark.

In the 1970s a family of seven was attacked by sharks when they abandoned their yacht in a storm off the coast of Florida, USA. Three of them were bitten, though fortunately two of them survived. One of the mistakes they made was not staying together in the water (thinking that if they separated they might be spotted more easily). Unfortunately, it simply encouraged the sharks to attack them.

Shark safety

These are the parts of the world where sharks are most likely to be found:

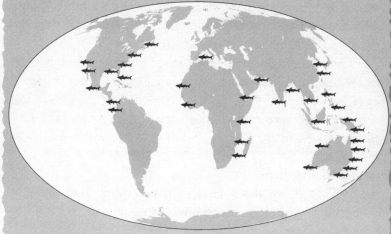

If you should find yourself in one of these areas, here are some tips:

● Avoid places where sharks are likely to look for food:
  • where people are fishing (the bait can attract sharks);
  • where waste is dumped into the sea.

- Swim in a large group – the more people together, the less likely one person is to be attacked.
- Don't swim after dark because some species of shark may come into the shallow water at this time.
- Keep away from areas where the depth suddenly changes, e.g. near a deep channel by the shore.
- Don't wear bright clothes or attachments that might interest a nosy shark.
- Don't swim if you have an open wound or are bleeding in any way, because sharks are attracted to even small amounts of blood.

Shark facts

– Most shark attacks take place in warm (above 21°C) sea water.

– The largest sharks are not always the most dangerous. Some sharks of only 1 m in length have attacked people, while some of the largest sharks only feed on fish.

– Shark attacks have occasionally taken place in rivers; the furthest one recorded inland was nearly 100 miles (160 km) up a river in Iran!

– In an average year more people are struck by lightning than are bitten by a shark.

Pushed to the limit

Often, sailing down the Atlantic, Knox-Johnston had found it quite boring being alone. But there was no time to be bored in the Southern Ocean!

Here he met severe storms. *Suhaili* was badly battered and the self-steering gear was damaged. But he made repairs as best he could and continued. His radio was broken too, so he could not send messages. He managed to make it safely round the Horn. Now they were on the homeward leg!

Illness

Soon it was the sailor, not the yacht, who was suffering. Knox-Johnston started having very bad stomach pains. Because he was now back among the shipping lanes, he tried to get help from another vessel, but they all ignored his signals.

If he had been helped, he would have been disqualified. His pains got better and on 22 April 1969 he sailed into Falmouth, England, his starting point. He had been at sea for 313 days.

Knox-Johnston was the only sailor to finish the Golden Globe and to circumnavigate the world according to its rules. He received the prize money and the trophy. But when the news of Crowhurst's tragic suicide came through, Knox-Johnston donated the £5,000 to the Crowhurst Appeal Fund.

The Golden Globe had been a race of excitements, triumphs, and tragedies. It had shown the great strains and stresses that can be inflicted on a person who sets out to sail round the world entirely alone.

OTHER GREAT SAILING FIRSTS

Over the next few years more and more people became inspired to sail round the world alone to try and break Knox-Johnston's record or to go against the direction of the main winds and currents of the Southern Ocean. See the timeline on pages 135–136 for more details of some of these.

Round-the-world races

Now racing round the world in a yacht has turned into a regular sport!

Although yachts and equipment may always be improving, the terrible storms in the Southern Ocean and the varied, often unpredictable, weather conditions elsewhere will always prove a challenge to sailors.

There are now many round-the-world races, for both crewed

yachts and for single-handers. Here are details of just a few:

The Whitbread Race

The Whitbread has proved to be an exciting race for crewed yachts of 12 people. The yachts sail eastwards in 'legs' to set ports. The race lasts about eight months. The Whitbread has taken place about every four years since the very first race in 1973, which started from Portsmouth, England. There were 17 starters and the winning yacht took 144 days.

The sailors have to be tough and committed. Records are often broken in the Whitbread for speed, distance and time. In the 1989–90 race, one of the crews achieved a new kind of record. *Maiden* (skippered by Tracy Edwards, 27, British) had the first-ever all-female crew to sail round the world!

The race has been run by the British Royal Naval Association, with sponsorship from a British brewery, Whitbread – hence its name. But the next Whitbread Race will be called the Volvo Ocean Race! This is because the car manufacturers, Volvo, have now taken over sponsorship of the race. Watch out for details in the press about this race in the year 2001 and beyond.

Sponsors

Sponsors are people or companies who provide money for many sports in return for the publicity it gives them. Top-class yacht racing is very expensive, so the people involved are always looking for ways of raising money. Often, racing yachts are named after their most important sponsors and/or carry sponsors' names and logos on their sails and hulls.

Calling non-sailors!

People who take part in round-the-world races are usually very experienced sailors. However, in the early 1990s, Chay Blyth (the first person to sail solo, non-stop, westwards round the world) linked up with the company British Steel to set up the British Steel Challenge. In this race, 10 yachts, all exactly the same, went round the world westwards.

This was also an opportunity for people who had no experience at all to sail round the world! Blyth wanted to give everyone the chance to take part in round-the-world sailing. To apply, you had to:

- be aged between 20 and 60
- show you could raise money for your voyage
- pass the selection test

The people who were accepted were those who Blyth thought had the right attitude and would work well as part of a team in both the good and bad times. There then were days, weekends and whole weeks of training. The 1992–3 British Steel Challenge was a great success, with many ordinary people achieving something extraordinary! In 1996–7 the race was called the BT Global Challenge after its new sponsors, British Telecom. There are more to come!

But what about races to sail alone round the world?

IN DANGER OF DYING — ALONE

Perhaps the greatest sea challenge of all nowadays for an extreme adventurer is the Vendée Globe, a single-handed, non-stop, round-the-world race. It starts from the Atlantic coast of the Vendée region of France. The course goes round the three southernmost capes of the world – Good Hope, Leeuwin and the Horn – and then back to France. It takes about eight months.

During this race the sailor has to pit his or her wits against

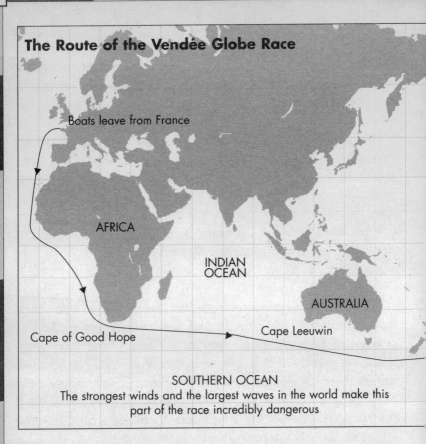

The Route of the Vendée Globe Race

Boats leave from France

AFRICA

INDIAN
OCEAN

AUSTRALIA

Cape of Good Hope

Cape Leeuwin

SOUTHERN OCEAN
The strongest winds and the largest waves in the world make this
part of the race incredibly dangerous

the great Southern Ocean. Two thirds of the race is spent here
– an area where the skies are usually grey and threatening,
where the winds are incredibly strong, the waves and swell
enormous … and land is a very, very long way away.

EXTREME FACTS
OCEAN STORMS

These can blow up in any sea but the great Southern Ocean
is known (and respected) for being a particularly dangerous
place for the most terrible storms. Their features include:

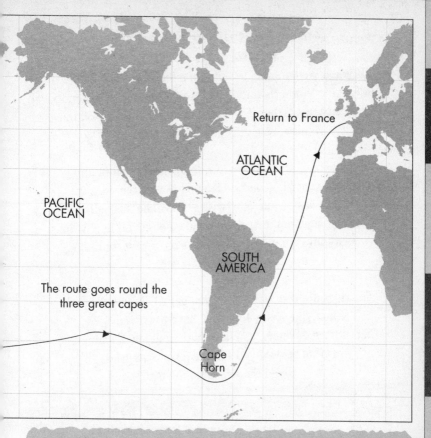

Return to France

ATLANTIC
OCEAN

PACIFIC
OCEAN

SOUTH
AMERICA

The route goes round the
three great capes

Cape
Horn

• Wild winds – these can reach up to 320 km/hr.

• Giant waves – the winds whip the waves up to an enormous height, as much as 35 m at times. These can cover, and even overturn your yacht.

Advice for the sailor

If the winds are really strong and the waves enormous, the best thing to do is to reduce the sail area as much as possible, go down below and sit the storm out. But be careful – if you take the sails down altogether your boat can end up being tossed around like a cork.

Rules for sailing round the world non-stop

If you are attempting to sail round the world you must follow the World Sailing Speed Record Council's general rules (see page 12), but if you plan to do it non-stop you must also 'be totally self-maintained':

- Nothing at all – no water, food, equipment or any kind of repair kit – can be taken on to the boat once the voyage has begun, otherwise you will be disqualified
- You can anchor the yacht, but must not get off at any time
- No physical help at all is allowed, except for radio communications

The rules are very strict, so if you get a hole in your yacht and, like Knox-Johnston, have to fix it in shark-infested waters, you have to do it alone. It's tough, isn't it? Could you survive a solo, non-stop, round-the-world sailing trip?

Sailors setting out on the Vendée Globe know that they are perhaps facing death. They know that throughout the voyage the dangers will be many. They consider battling against the elements in the Southern Ocean as the greatest challenge of all.

The first Vendée Globe was in 1989–90. Only 7 out of the 13 competitors finished. In the 1992–3 race only 6 out of 14 made it. One competitor disappeared in the Atlantic and another had to be rescued south of Australia.

In the 1996–7 race there were 16 starters. Among them was British sailor Tony Bullimore, aged 58 – who was described as a 'sea-dog' by his wife. Bullimore was experienced and tough. He was going to need all his inner reserves of strength for what was about to happen to him.

TRAPPED!

On 5 January 1997 Bullimore's yacht, *Global Exide Challenger*, overturned in very high seas 3,300 km south-west of Western Australia. It all happened very quickly.

The yacht was being tossed around by a wild storm and Bullimore was taking a rest below deck in a chair, with a cup of tea, when he heard a sudden loud crack. His yacht started to roll over very fast.

He didn't have time to do anything. It was only two or three seconds before she was upside-down in the water – probably as long as it's taken you to read this paragraph.

Bullimore found himself trapped in an air-pocket in the cabin. He was sitting on the ceiling. The floor was now above him. Although there was hardly any water in here with him, through a window he could see nothing but wild foaming ocean. What was he going to do?

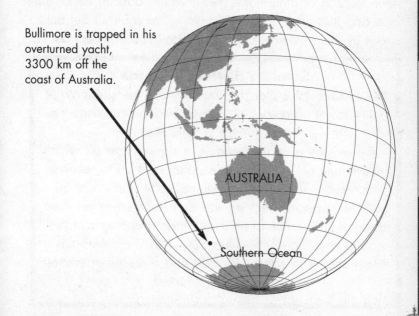

Bullimore is trapped in his overturned yacht, 3300 km off the coast of Australia.

AUSTRALIA

Southern Ocean

Self-righting yachts

Yachts in the Vendée Globe are meant to be self-righting. This means that if they capsize they should automatically come back to the correct, upright position. But it seems that the *Global Exide Challenger* hit an object under the water that broke the keel. This is why she turned completely upside-down and stayed there.

Most people would have panicked, but Bullimore didn't. He sat on the ceiling and considered the situation. Even activating his distress beacon was a problem because it wouldn't work inside the hull. How could he get it outside without letting a flood of water in as well?

A few hours later one of the yacht's windows smashed and solved this problem – but caused a few others. Bullimore pushed the beacon out through the broken window, hoping against hope that it would bob up to the surface and that the signal would work. He couldn't get out to check because he would probably have been swept away.

Satellite distress beacons

Nowadays if a sailor gets into trouble, he/she may be able to set off a special distress beacon that uses the technology of satellites.

By switching on the beacon, a signal is set off which alerts one of 14 worldwide stations set up to receive such calls. The signal is automatically sent every 50 seconds. Special tracking satellites each cover an area about 3,000 miles (5,000 km) wide and they can pinpoint your signal to within 800–1,800 m. With this information you can be located and a rescue operation will then be mounted.

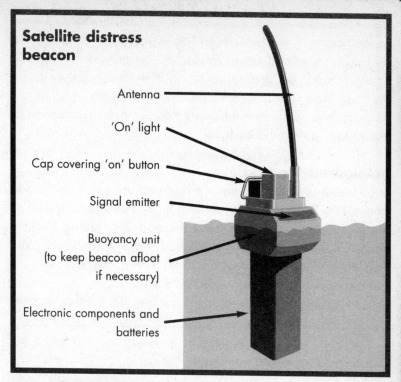

Satellite distress beacon

Antenna

'On' light

Cap covering 'on' button

Signal emitter

Buoyancy unit
(to keep beacon afloat
if necessary)

Electronic components and
batteries

Diving challenge

The broken window meant that sea water had now poured in to the compartment, up to the 'water-line' outside. This water rolled around inside as the yacht was tossed about in the sea. Bullimore found his survival suit and put it on. He greatly regretted that he hadn't brought the one which included covering for hands and feet.

He decided to try and free the life-raft. It was still in its box under the deck but tangled up among ropes. If he could release it, it would be ready for use if the yacht suddenly sank.

Bullimore took a deep breath and made a brave dive into the freezing water to try and cut it free. With one hand, he hung on to the life-raft's rope as he cut away at the other ropes. Around him, his yacht was being hurled about by the fierce ocean. It was an almost impossible task. After a while he had to stop and return to his little air-pocket in the cabin to dry himself out and try to warm himself up. But he didn't give up. After about two hours, he tried again. And again. And again … Bullimore definitely had the determination to be a survivor, but would he live?

Bullimore's 'Bolt Hole'

In between his dives, Bullimore huddled on a little shelf, only about 1 m long, 0.5 m wide and high. He had strapped up some netting, like a hammock, to stop him falling into the water as the yacht rolled. He called this his 'bolt hole'. This was how he stayed out of the chilly water that was swirling around below him in the upturned yacht.

If he was going to keep himself alive, he needed to keep

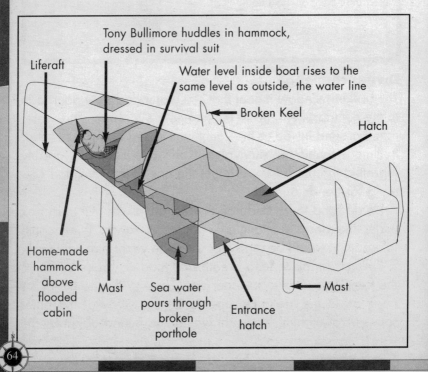

Tony Bullimore huddles in hammock, dressed in survival suit

Liferaft

Water level inside boat rises to the same level as outside, the water line

Broken Keel

Hatch

Home-made hammock above flooded cabin

Mast

Sea water pours through broken porthole

Entrance hatch

Mast

his energy up. The only thing he had to eat was some chocolate. He kept it in his pocket as there was nowhere else to put it. It quickly became wet and salty, so it tasted pretty awful. But it was definitely better than nothing.

For water he had a survival water-maker (which could filter sea water into drinking water, but only for a limited period). The chocolate and the water-maker helped to keep him going. His survival suit (also known as a dry suit) cut down heat loss from his body.

But none of these things is any good if there is no chance of rescue. The freezing cold conditions meant that he was getting the symptoms of frost-bite in his fingers and toes. He knew that perhaps his greatest danger was hypothermia. Would he be found before he died?

EXTREME FACTS
THE FREEZING SEA

Hypothermia is one of the greatest dangers for a sailor. This is when your body temperature becomes very low – caused by extreme cold or being immersed in water below 20°C. If left untreated, you will become unconscious and perhaps die. The chances of staying alive for more than a few minutes in the freezing waters of the Southern Ocean are very low.

Many of the people on the *Titanic*, which sank on 15 April 1912, did not drown but died of hypothermia in the icy waters of the North Atlantic Ocean.

Frostbite happens when extreme cold causes body tissues – especially fingers, toes, nose and ears – to freeze. This is because the body is trying to conserve heat at the centre to protect the vital organs, like the heart. The affected areas become very painful, then they go numb and start to die. The skin feels hard and stiff to touch. If left untreated, the flesh will become black and begin to rot. You will only survive if the affected area is cut away or amputated (cut off).

Many sailors have suffered from frost-bite when working on deck in freezing conditions. If they are not careful, they can end up losing parts of their fingers.

But Bullimore had great strength of mind. The sort of person who takes part in this race is going to be tough and is used to being on their own. If they couldn't cope with the stress caused by the terrible danger, they wouldn't have entered the most gruelling race in the world. They would be sitting at home safe and sound.

What Bullimore couldn't know was that, far away from his pitching, upturned yacht, things were happening. His distress beacon signal *had* been picked up and the emergency services in Australia informed. They were aware of the terrible conditions in the area surrounding the yacht. The winds were over 100 km/hr, the air temperature 1°C and the water temperature about 5°C. Not only were the chances of someone surviving there very poor, a rescue operation would be extremely difficult to mount in the storm-tossed seas.

Wind Speed
The speed and force of the wind is usually measured on the Beaufort Scale. There are 12 grades of wind speed on the scale. Here are a few of them:
Force 0 (0 km/hr)
Total calm. On land, chimney smoke rises straight. At sea,

lack of wind makes it impossible to sail.
Force 5 (30–39 km/hr)
Fresh breeze. On land, small trees sway. At sea, a good strong sailing wind but sailors may need to use smaller sails to keep control of their yachts.
Force 10 (88–101 km/hr)
Storm. Not common on land. Trees will be uprooted, buildings damaged. At sea, a serious danger of yachts being capsized.
Force 12 (118+ km/hr)
Total devastation and threat to life on land and at sea.

Rescue at last?

Twenty-four hours after Bullimore first activated his distress signal, a Royal Australian Air Force (RAAF) plane searching for him spotted his upturned yacht and flew over it. The crew could see no sign of Bullimore or his life-raft. They feared the worst.

But suddenly the listeners in the plane heard a new kind of signal coming from the yacht. It was a different type of sound. The switch over could not have been made automatically: it could only have been set off by a human being! This meant that Bullimore must be still alive! There was great excitement. The race was on to rescue the old 'sea-dog' ...

A lonely man

Bullimore thought he heard the sound of an aircraft overhead but didn't know if his mind was playing tricks. He knew that if it was an aircraft it must be looking for him. He had to fight the very great temptation to swim out from under the yacht. However horrible his hell hole might be, he knew that once he left its security he would never be able to get back to it. The risk was too great. If his tiny bobbing body wasn't seen by the aircraft, he would never survive in the freezing waters without a liferaft.

So he had decided to change the style of the distress signal instead. This had probably saved his life.

As he heard what he thought was the plane fly away, he felt even more alone. He didn't know if his yacht had been spotted. He didn't know if his changed signal had been picked up. Just the idea that there had probably been people near by made the wait even more difficult and the loneliness even greater.

Action elsewhere

What he didn't know was that the Australian rescue services were in touch with his yacht builder in Britain. Details of the compartment design inside *Global Exide Challenger* were being faxed to Australia to make it easier for the rescue services to cut into the hull. People were trying to work out how much air he might have left in the upturned yacht. But for Bullimore this was one worry he didn't have, because air was coming in through the broken window (with water), and also through the small gap where the keel had broken.

Tap, tap, tapping ...

HMAS *Adelaide* set off from Western Australia to try and rescue him. Another plane flew over and dropped electronic noise makers and sonar buoys (equipment which picks up sounds) into the sea. By now the weather had got even worse and the air temperature had dropped to -2°C.

Crew on the RAAF plane now heard, via the sonar buoys, the sound of human tapping from inside the hull of the yacht. Towards midday on 9 January 1997, the *Adelaide*'s crew spotted the upturned hull of *Global Exide Challenger* in the wild rough waters. The captain had three choices:

1 Send out divers in a rubber dinghy;
2 Turn the yacht over with the crane on the *Adelaide*;
3 Send out a team to cut through the hull.

At first the captain sent out a dinghy with divers, while the *Adelaide* circled the yacht and sounded her horn. The divers called out, 'Is anyone there?' They hammered on the hull. They heard Bullimore hammer back. 'Mr Bullimore is alive,' they radioed back to the ship. 'We are in contact with him!'

The divers managed to get a rope over the hull and were preparing to cut through it. Then, suddenly, to everyone's surprise, Bullimore popped up in the water on the other side!

Although the waters were freezing and rough, he now was certain that there were people outside the yacht to rescue him. He knew it was no longer a risk to come out from under the yacht. It had been a *very* long four-day wait.

Tony Bullimore's head pops up from the stern of his yacht (on far right)!

Bullimore was pulled into the dinghy, wrapped in a silver foil blanket and taken to HMAS *Adelaide*. His feet were frost-bitten and he was suffering from hypothermia. He was covered in cuts and bruises, he had lost the tip of a little finger in a hatch, and he was exhausted – but he was alive! After an hour in the ship's sick bay, he just wanted to talk and talk about his experiences. He couldn't thank his rescuers enough. 'They were all heroes,' he said.

EXTREME FACTS
BOAT TROUBLE

If your yacht is in serious trouble and
you need to be rescued this is what you should do:

- Let off your distress beacon
- Stay with your yacht for as long as you can
- Have your life-raft ready, but don't get into it unless absolutely necessary. It is much easier for a rescuer to spot a yacht than a tiny raft in wild, rough seas
- Don't panic! Experts say that it's not just physical strength and stamina that is needed to survive in extreme situations, but also the ability to keep calm and to have the determination to believe that you will succeed. Bullimore had all these qualities.

A modern rescue

This was the first time a rescue like this had taken place so far south. Ten years earlier it couldn't have happened and Bullimore would almost certainly have died. Modern technology, such as the up-to-date distress-signalling system, had made it possible to find his yacht.

Clinging to life

About the same time that Tony Bullimore was going through his terrible ordeal, rescues were going on in the Southern Ocean to save two other competitors in the race.

The same terrible storm had overturned the yacht of a French competitor, Thiery Dubois, who had been 500 nautical miles north of Bullimore. Dubois had also sent out a distress signal.

The next day Dubois, wearing a survival suit, was sighted clinging to his upturned yacht in very rough seas. He hung on there for 24 hours before he managed to scramble on to a life-raft dropped by a RAAF plane.

HMAS *Adelaide* had then got near enough to send out a helicopter to rescue him. With Dubois safe, the ship hurried on to find Bullimore. Dubois was ready to welcome him when he came on board. Both men had a lot to be thankful for!

Air-Sea rescue

The stages of an air-sea rescue usually follow a set procedure, taking place in three steps:

1. A plane drops the air-sea rescue pack to the sailor(s). This is a chain of four packages connected by rope. Two packages contain life-rafts and the other two are survival packs containing emergency supplies.

2. The sailor opens up one of the life-raft packages and inflates it, climbing inside for shelter. The survival packs will keep him/her going until rescue arrives. Now all he/she can do is wait.

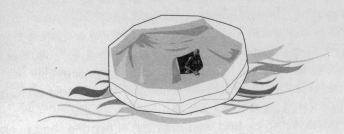

3. Finally, rescue will arrive. Dubois was airlifted by helicopter. However, another competitor was rescued by a nearby yacht (see next page).

The air-sea rescue pack includes the following items:
- ❏ torches
- ❏ pocket knives
- ❏ whistle (to alert people to your location)
- ❏ signalling mirrors (used to catch the light and signal over longer distances)
- ❏ survival blankets
- ❏ first-aid kits & manuals
- ❏ insect repellent
- ❏ sunscreen
- ❏ lip chap stick
- ❏ sun goggles
- ❏ toilet paper
- ❏ drinking water
- ❏ tubes of condensed milk
- ❏ emergency fishing kits
- ❏ packets of marine safety matches (damp proof)
- ❏ 2 packs of playing cards

Rough work!

A second dramatic rescue had taken place a just few days previously. Early on Boxing Day morning another Frenchman, Raphael Dinelli, had set off a distress beacon. The race organizers contacted a fellow competitor in the race, British man Pete Goss. He was the nearest vessel to Dinelli – and his best chance of survival.

Goss had also been suffering with the storm and his yacht, *Aqua Quorum*, had capsized many times, but luckily, so far, she had always righted herself. If he set out to try and rescue Dinelli, he would have to turn back. He would be giving up on the race. But Goss knew that he had to go: it's a sailor's instinct to help someone in trouble on the sea (deep down sailors know that it could be them next time).

Goss was told on his radio that Dinelli had managed to get into a life-raft dropped by a rescue plane, just minutes before his yacht had sunk.

Goss eventually spotted the life-raft and managed to heave Dinelli on board his yacht. He lay stiff and freezing on deck, with cold, colourless hands and feet. But he was alive. Dinelli was a lucky man. Eleven days later they reached Australia.

A tragedy

The three men had all survived. But there *was* one terrible tragedy during the race. Canadian Gerry Roufs went missing south-west of Cape Horn on 7 January 1997. Ships in the area and other competitors went to look for him, but there was no sign of his yacht. It wasn't until six months later that the empty wreck of his yacht was found drifting off the coast of Chile. No one knew what had happened to him. His body has never been found.

Food for a non-stop sailor

An enormous amount of food is needed for a non-stop, eight-month sail. Most of it is dried food, to save weight. It is cooked on a stove, with water added, to make a hot meal. The food needs to be nutritious (i.e. healthy food, not junk food!) and it needs to provide the right amount of energy for the place in the world where the sailor is. The colder it is, the more energy you need.

Bags of bags!

Vendée Globe sailor Goss took food for 120 days, worked out into a 6-day menu cycle (so Sunday's meal wouldn't always be the same).

• Each meal was individually packed, then put into daily bags. These were packed into larger six-day bags, which contained other weekly essentials, such as toilet paper, matches and vitamin tablets.
• The bags were numbered and put in an order that meant he would have the right amount of calories for wherever he was on his trip. In the hot Tropics he would need about 3,500 calories per day, but in the cold Southern Ocean more like 5,500 calories. (People leading an everyday life need 2,000–3,000 calories a day.)
• There were also special food bags for stormy weather when nothing could be cooked.

Goss's parents prepared all his food and bags for him and packed a surprise meal for every 14th day (as well as Christmas Day and his birthday), with some treats!

It's a dog's life!

While sailing, Goss ate his food out of a dog bowl. The wide base stopped the bowl overturning, the high sides kept the food in and the bowl seemed to keep food warm for longer than an ordinary plate. Extreme explorers are very practical!

MILLENNIUM SAILING RECORDS

These new records were set at the end of the twentieth century. Will they be broken in the new millennium?

Fastest westwards, solo, non-stop

The current fastest westwards, solo, non-stop record was set in 1994. Sailing against the main winds of the Southern Ocean, British man Mike Golding arrived back at Southampton, England, on 7 May 1994, 161 days after he had left!

Smallest sailing boat

Imagine going around the world in a yacht just 3.6 m (11 ft 10 in) long! Well, that's what Australian Serge Testa did! He left Brisbane, Australia, in 1984 and arrived back there 500 days later, in 1986.

Youngest solo non-stop sailor

The youngest person to sail around the world non-stop is eighteen-year-old Jesse Martin, who returned to Melbourne, Australia after sailing around the globe solo and completely unassisted in his 11-metre yacht. He was greeted by thousands of supporters when he arrived back at port in October 1999. Jesse had had a few hairy moments along the way, including narrowly escaping a collision with a huge tanker!

The Jules Verne Trophy

This is awarded for sailing round the world non-stop in less than 80 days – the fictional Phileas Fogg's travelling time (see page 13). There is no restriction on the type of yacht or number of crew. Sailing is eastwards, because this is quickest way to go (see page 42).

In 1997 Olivier de Kersauson and his crew, on *Sport Elec*, set a new record of 71 days, 14 hours, 22 minutes and 8 seconds.

Modern technology means it is becoming possible to sail yachts faster and faster. And 'The Race' is putting this to the test at the beginning of the new millenium.

'The Race'!

'The Race' is open to any yacht of any size with any number of crew. It is part of France's millennium celebrations. On 31 December 2000 the biggest and fastest yachts ever built set off from the Straits of Gibraltar to circle the globe non-stop as fast as possible. There will be many excitements and dangers – and records, like the Jules Verne, will probably be broken. Some new types of boats and sails have been designed especially for 'The Race'. If they do well, some sailing techniques might change altogether.

FLYING HIGH

Flying round the world has never been as simple as it sounds. For the very early pilots there were all kinds of problems to consider, including:

- finding suitable landing and stopover points.
- arranging refuelling points.

Unlike today, there were very few airports and landing strips around the world. Also many of the early planes didn't have very reliable instruments, so it was extremely important to wait for the right weather conditions.

These can all still be problems for modern-day pilots, but planning a round-the-world flight is much less difficult for them.

However, world circumnavigation has not always been the first aim of pilots and aircraft designers. Aviation records have tended to focus more on speed and technological developments. But there *are* exciting records set for circumnavigation by flight. Here are some of the most significant ones before 1986 when the ultimate – and one of the most dangerous – of all circumnavigation challenges was made by aeroplane – a non-stop flight round the world without *any* refuelling!

FIRST FLIGHTS ROUND THE WORLD

By plane

The first circumnavigation of the world by aeroplane was completed on 28 September 1924 by two US Army Air Service, open-cockpit, single-engine biplanes. They took 175 days to cover 26,193 miles (42,152 km), having left Seattle, Washington state, USA, on 6 April. There were 69 short hops and a whole range of support facilities. The flying time was 371 hours, 11 minutes and they set a record that was to stand for over 70 years (see page 93).

By airship

Between 8 and 29 August 1929 the German airship the *Graf Zeppelin* circled the world in 21 days, 5 hours and 31 minutes, flying to and from New Jersey, USA. The total distance covered was over 21,870 miles (35,200 km).

First solo

The first man to fly solo round the world – or at least round the Northern Hemisphere – was an American from Texas, called Wiley Post, who was blind in one eye. He set out on 15 July 1933 and flew eastwards across the Atlantic, Europe, the USSR and over the Pacific to cross Alaska and Canada. He did the journey in 7 days, 18 hours and 49 minutes, with stops. He covered 15,596 miles (25,100 km).

First solo woman

The first woman to fly round the world solo was Jerrie Mock, 37, who returned to Columbus, Ohio, USA on 17 April 1964 after completing 23,103 miles (37,180 km).

The flight took 29 days, with 21 stopovers. Her plane was called *Spirit of Columbus*. Jerrie flew according to the new FAI rules (see page 12).

Women had an advantage over men in early long-distance flights because they were usually lighter, a major plus when weight had to be kept to a minimum to save fuel.

First non-stop

In 1949 a US Air Force Boeing B-50, *Lucky Lady II*, took 93 hours to go round the world. It was refuelled in flight – the first time this had been done. The intention was to impress the Russians with the advancement and skill of American air power. This record was soon broken by larger planes called B-52s, but they still had to be refuelled in flight.

THE VICTORIOUS *VOYAGER*

The idea: To fly an aeroplane the whole way round the world without *any* refuelling.

This required a purpose-built machine which could carry all the fuel necessary. It had to be light because the heavier the plane, the more fuel it would need. This aircraft wouldn't break the round-the-world speed record because it would have to fly at a steady, slow speed to preserve fuel – but it was a revolutionary idea, and, if it succeeded, it would be a world first!

The people (all Americans)

The crew:

• Jeana Yeager, 34, had trained to be the first woman in space.

• Dick Rutan, 49, had flown over 100 combat missions as a US fighter pilot during the Vietnam War.

The designer:

• Burt Rutan, younger brother of Dick. He had first shown Jeana and Dick his sketch for this special plane on a table napkin at dinner in 1980.

The aircraft

Voyager was built of a strong, yet light, material. She was really a flying fuel tank (for 5,450 litres of fuel!), with two engines (front and rear) and just a tiny, uncomfortable cockpit only 1 m wide and 2.25 m long. It would be like living and working in a telephone box!

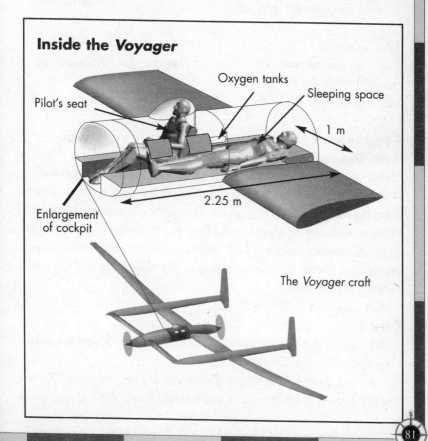

Inside the *Voyager*

Oxygen tanks

Sleeping space

Pilot's seat

1 m

2.25 m

Enlargement of cockpit

The *Voyager* craft

The planning

Voyager took six years to plan and build. During this time the team of supporters and workers grew and sponsors were found to finance the huge cost of the project.

The tests

Yeager and Rutan took *Voyager* on 67 trial flights. On these flights they tested everything from the landing gear to food rations, and from oxygen supplies to their very basic toilet facilities – a tube for peeing into and a bag that had to be stuck on to your bottom for solid matter! They also tested parachutes, survival equipment and rafts.

The weight

Not only the aircraft, but also all the provisions and supplies on board had to be as light as possible. Yeager even had her long hair cut to help reduce the weight!

The take-off

Take-off was from Edwards Air Force Base, in the Mojave Desert on the west coast of the USA, on 14 December 1986.

Everyone was tense as *Voyager* sped down the runway, passing families, friends, ground crew and press. If the ground crew saw a fire or a fuel leak, they were to call 'Abort, abort!' over the radio. Luckily they didn't need to. The runway was more than a mile and a half long. They needed this distance to reach take-off speed.

Day 1

Safely up in the air, *Voyager* flew off westwards, in the direction of the Pacific Ocean.

In a less technical moment they stuck a piece of paper to the control panel with the days written on it, so they could mark

The crew of Voyager stand next to a picture of their craft, which shows its unusual design.

them off – like a chart showing the countdown to the end of a school term!

Daily life on *Voyager*

Food and drink

All food was pre-cooked and put into sealed packages for heating up on the rear engine's radiator. An immersion heater was used to heat liquids.

They took 50 litres of water, weighing 40 kg, as well as fruit juices for energy. The water was stored in individual plastic bags (each about a cup's worth) into which they stuck a straw to drink. It was important for them to drink a lot of water so they didn't get dehydrated (see page 109).

Clothes

They both wore jogging suits and cotton underwear, which was practical and comfortable. (Aviators wear cotton rather than synthetic material because it catches fire less quickly in the event of an accident.)

Washing

They had skin and hair cleansers with them. They found cleaning their teeth always made them feel better!

Exercise

They had a enormous rubber band to help them stretch and exercise their joints in the cramped space.

Day 2

On day two *Voyager* had to divert slightly north off her planned course to try and avoid the worst of Typhoon Marge, a tropical storm that had been developing in the Pacific. The typhoon was hundreds of miles wide, and if they kept on the edge of it the strong winds could help them move faster. But if they misjudged and came in too close, *Voyager* could be ripped to pieces! The typhoon shifted and they had to change their course, but they got through.

Hurricanes, typhoons and cyclones

A hurricane is a tropical storm, usually about 400 miles (650 km) across, with strong winds – up to 200 km/hr – and carrying very heavy rain. The winds circle round a calm 'eye' or centre. Hurricanes in the north-west Pacific are known as typhoons; in the southern Pacific and Indian Oceans they are called cyclones.

Day 3

As they flew over the Philippines, they hit bad turbulence. Next the autopilot failed! Luckily they had brought a spare one. But as they fixed it in place they felt gloomy – it was far too early for this piece of equipment to stop working. If the replacement broke too, they'd be in big trouble. The concentration and commitment to fly the plane manually would not be possible as they grew more tired.

Flying *Voyager* required a lot of effort. Even the person who wasn't piloting could not go to sleep for long. As well as flying the plane, there was an enormous amount to be done in the cockpit all the time:

– constant checks on the temperature, the oil, the engine cooler, the onboard computer and fuel use

– transferring fuel from the various tanks when needed

– writing up the log, recording position, speed, winds, fuel transfers, etc.

– communicating on the radio

> **Automatic pilot (autopilot)**
> The automatic pilot is a system which flies the aeroplane
> along a set course at a set height. But the pilot still has to be
> alert to changing weather conditions and alter the direction
> or height, if needed.

Day 4

Voyager was now flying over the vast Indian Ocean (see map on pages 90–91). This is an area where small but sudden storms arise and radio contact is often bad. They had to take a more northerly course than they had intended because of the weather.

In the cabin the pilot sat in front. Swapping around involved climbing over each other. The trip was far from comfortable and it was also very noisy.

Day 5

Voyager was now nearing the coast of Africa. So far so good, despite the weather. They were about halfway through their journey! Only 11,250 miles (18,000 km) left to go!

Flying through more storms, they passed over Kenya (they had been told to avoid Somalia because of the civil war, in case they got shot down by mistake). Now their route lay over some high mountains and the Great Rift Valley, famous for terrible thunderstorms. They had been advised not to fly further north because of other wars.

As *Voyager* started climbing to cross over Mount Kenya, Rutan and Yeager had to put on oxygen masks. The storms here were severe, often throwing *Voyager* around so wildly that the two of them were bounced off the sides and roof of the cockpit again and again. They were battered and bruised.

Oxygen crisis!

Suddenly Rutan, who was piloting, realized that Yeager had not said anything for a while. He could see she was lying in a strange position, her body all hunched up. He called her name over the intercom but there was no reply. He managed to reach behind him and touch her. She was cold.

Flying *Voyager* with one hand, he lent back and shook her. Nothing happened. He shook her again and she suddenly jolted up, nearly hitting the roof. She seemed dazed and complained that she had a bad headache and wanted to sleep. It was the lack of oxygen that had made her like this. It was a very dangerous situation, but they had to keep going; Rutan couldn't fly any lower or even land among these high mountains.

Rutan too was feeling pretty giddy. But he had to keep flying the aircraft at 6,000 m to clear the mountains, trying to avoid all the storms, *and* keep shaking Yeager regularly to make sure she didn't become a corpse. What would he do if she died?

Eventually, as the plains came into view, Rutan let *Voyager* descend. Yeager now began to stir, but she still had a throbbing headache, felt very sick and found it difficult to stay awake.

Freezing feet

Rutan then realized he could not feel his feet. He had been concentrating so hard on flying the plane through the frightening storms that he hadn't noticed them getting cold and wet at the high altitude. He took off his slippers and his two pairs of socks. His feet were white and waxy. He warmed them up by feeding the hose from the heater into a little tent he had made with a blanket. It took three hours of wiggling and massaging to get feeling back into them.

EXTREME FACTS
OXYGEN DANGERS

The higher up you go, the less oxygen there is in the air, so it becomes more difficult to breathe. This isn't usually a problem nowadays in commercial planes because oxygen is circulated throughout the cabin. But if you ever suffer from a severe shortage of oxygen, you can get hypoxia. This can have the following effects:

- feeling short of breath
- feeling drowsy and confused
- fainting
- lips, tongue, fingertips and toes go blue (this is because the body is saving your blood supply for vital organs like the brain and heart)

Eventually, you may become unconscious.

Day 6 – Warning!

The red oil warning light came on at a bad moment. They were 165 miles (265 km) away from the African coast over the Atlantic Ocean and Rutan was in the back, about to go to the toilet! He had his parachute harness off, his trousers down and was going to attach a special stick-on plastic bag to his bottom. Yeager always put up a little curtain when she was doing this but he didn't usually bother.

Rutan stuck the plastic bag to the ceiling and scrambled madly to get his trousers back up. Then he squirmed frantically to put his parachute harness back on. It usually took about 10 minutes. But he had to be as quick as possible. If there was a serious problem, they would have to bale out (jump out) immediately.

The red light meant the oil temperature was too high. Yeager's first move, as the pilot, was to push Voyager's nose down so that as much air as possible would move through the radiators and start to cool the oil. At the back of the aircraft Rutan worked to do everything possible to cool the oil further. An engine problem over the ocean was very serious – not a good place to bale out.

After a nerve-racking half hour, the cooling efforts they had put into operation were starting to work. The oil light had gone out. Were Rutan and Yeager, and *Voyager*, going to survive this trip?

Day 9 – So near ... and yet so far

The adventures had continued, but they were still in the air and by day nine were flying up the Pacific coast of America again. They were on their way home!

Voyager faced very strong head winds, really slowing her down. If *Voyager* was slowed up too much there might not be enough fuel to complete the journey.

Suddenly the worry over fuel supplies was no longer important. There was something far worse to deal with ... *Voyager's* rear engine suddenly coughed and went dead.

Plummeting downwards

There was a horrible silence. Rutan and Yeager found themselves plummeting in a spiral, down towards the ground. In desperation they tried to restart either of the engines. Nothing happened. They kept trying, and trying ... for 90 terrifying seconds they dropped like a stone.

They had fallen 1,000 m before they managed to get an engine going. At the very last moment, Rutan levelled *Voyager* out. It had been the worst moment of the whole flight – a near disaster.

But they were still alive and *Voyager* was still flying! However, the fall had made fumes leak into the tiny cabin and they had to use oxygen masks again. In fact they used them for the rest of the journey as the oxygen helped to lessen their extreme tiredness as well.

On the right they could see lights as they flew up the coast of Mexico. Then they flew past Los Angeles, making their way back to the desert from where they had set off. Despite all the problems, they were probably going to make it!

The flight of *Voyager*

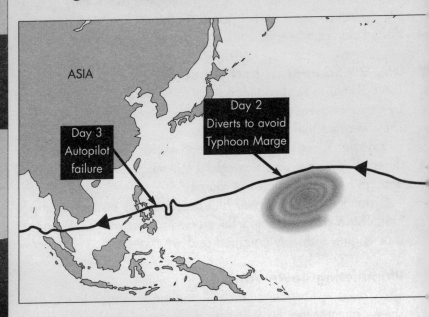

ASIA

Day 3
Autopilot
failure

Day 2
Diverts to avoid
Typhoon Marge

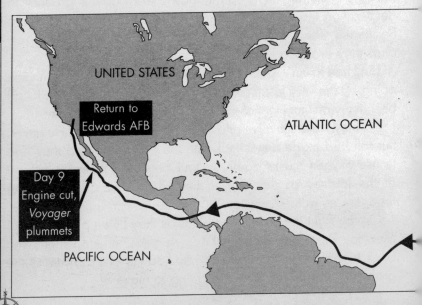

UNITED STATES

Return to
Edwards AFB

ATLANTIC OCEAN

Day 9
Engine cut,
Voyager
plummets

PACIFIC OCEAN

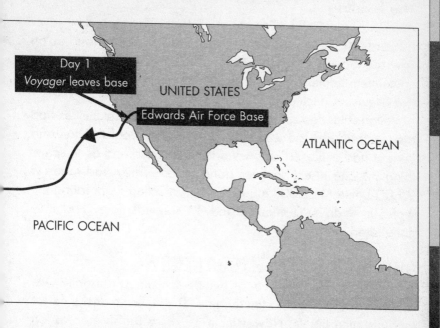

Day 1
Voyager leaves base

UNITED STATES

Edwards Air Force Base

ATLANTIC OCEAN

PACIFIC OCEAN

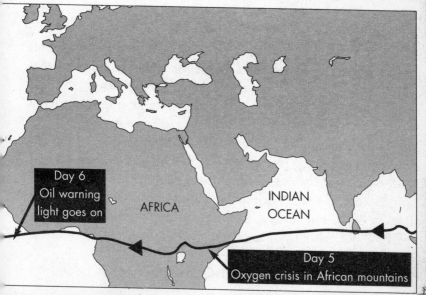

Day 6
Oil warning
light goes on

AFRICA

INDIAN
OCEAN

Day 5
Oxygen crisis in African mountains

The landing

At 7.32 a.m., 23 December 1986, *Voyager* flew over Edwards Air Force Base in a clear blue sky. Yeager and Rutan saw the crowds of people below who had turned out to welcome them home. The entire American nation was watching on live television, including the President!

Voyager landed at the base where many space shuttles had also landed. She too was now in the history books! Rutan and Yeager had achieved a new world record and had done something no one else had ever done before. They had made a 25,000 mile (40,000 km), non-stop, unfuelled flight round the world in 9 days, 3 minutes and 44 seconds. They had truly conquered the globe!

ONE MAN IN A MICROLIGHT

A microlight is a little one- or two-person aircraft (usually with an open cockpit) with a tiny engine. They are not designed for long-distance flights. However, in 1998, a British man, Brian Milton, aged 55, landed in England after a 121-day trip round the world!

He said that this landing was one of the 'hairiest' moments on his whole adventure because the winds and turbulence were really bad. They might have rolled the microlight over. 'It could have ruined the story,' he said. After he landed the microlight had to be held down to stop it being blown away!

Milton had set out to match the 80 day 'record' of the fictional Phileas Fogg (see page 13), but he had endless delays and problems on his trip which held him up. He hit blizzards in Alaska and fierce heat in the Middle East, which meant he had to carry out several emergency landings! Over Syria a military aircraft flew around his microlight when he entered the country's airspace, which was very frightening.

Delays with the Russian and Chinese authorities added an

extra 45 days on to his journey, so he had no chance of beating Mr Fogg.

However, Milton did break a real record – the one set in 1924 for flying round-the-world in an open-cockpit, single-engined aircraft. Maybe a microlight will beat Fogg yet!

Milton and co-pilot fly the microlight on a test run for the round-the-world record.

BALLOONING BATTLES

Ballooning can be a very dangerous sport. However, this hasn't stopped people from trying to be the first to travel round the world this way. At the end of the twentieth century, the battle to set the record was really hotting up.

Although the first manned balloon flight had taken place in 1783, 200 years later no manned hot-air balloon had managed to travel further than 600 miles (965 km). Over the next 15 years, as the twentieth century drew to a close, more and more sophisticated balloons were developed. Millionaires and rich companies invested a great deal of time, money and effort into producing the balloon – and the team – that would be the first to fly round the world. Several people died in their attempts.

Balloon technology

Modern balloons are very different from the old-fashioned models used in the early days of ballooning. These days, balloonists usually fly in sophisticated, pressurised capsules, which are attached to a helium-powered balloon.

A modern balloon and capsule design, based on the *ICO Global* model used by Richard Branson and his crew (see page 99).

Outer skin of balloon

A sphere contains helium gas, which 'lifts' the balloon

Hot air cone stops balloon descending when the outside air cools down at night

Capsule

Enlargement of capsule

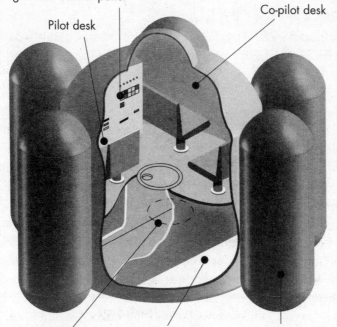

Flight deck control panel

Pilot desk

Co-pilot desk

Aircraft-style toilet – waste is recycled inside the capsule

Sleeping area has CD and video players

Fuel tank

Each balloon design is slightly different but most capsules have just enough space for a sleeping area and a toilet as well as the all-important control deck.

The balloon pilot sits at the control deck and uses computers and video cameras to navigate. Important controls are the altimeter and the rate of climb meter, which tell you how high up you are and how fast you are going up or down. The pilot also has control over the gas used to power the balloon, which is held in cyclinders. Radio contact with the balloon's control centre on the ground uses satellite links.

FIVE-MILE FALL

In August 1998, American millionaire Steve Fossett was in the middle of his fourth attempt to circumnavigate the world. He was flying solo and had already travelled 15,200 miles (24,500 km).

He was flying over the Pacific and was trying to make his way over the top of a line of thunderstorms when he got sucked down into one. This was to prove disastrous! His balloon, *Solo Spirit*, was torn by the force of the storm and started plunging from 29,000 ft (8,800 m) – more than 5 miles (8 km) up – towards the sea off the coast of Queensland, Australia.

Fossett thought he was going to die. In his desperation he tried to cut away the fuel tanks to reduce the weight. In the last 30 seconds before he hit the sea he managed to release several of the tanks, which gave the balloon a lift and made the impact a little less hard. This probably saved his life. Even so, his capsule immediately began to fill with water and the balloon caught fire.

Fosset was lucky enough to scramble into a life-raft. Or was he?

His life-raft was adrift in shark-infested waters in an area of dangerous reefs and enormous salt-water crocodiles. He set off two satellite distress beacons. The signals were picked up and three vessels in the area were diverted to help. In the mean time an aircraft dropped a life-raft near by with food and fresh water.

The waters Fossett had landed in were largely uncharted and, by now, it was growing dark. It would be a dangerous journey for any boat making her way towards him through the reefs. But the *Atlanta*, an Australian yacht, managed to locate and rescue him. Fossett had been afloat for 20 hours.

FURTHER FAILED ATTEMPTS

Fossett's close touch with death didn't put him off making further attempts to fly round the world by balloon. A rival, Briton Richard Branson, contacted him while he was still in the rescue boat off Australia and asked if he would like to join forces. Branson, another millionaire, had also made several attempts to hot-air balloon round the world.

Crash-landing

On his first attempt, Branson had crash-landed in the Algerian desert after only 23 hours and 400 miles (650 km). His co-pilot, Alex Ritchie, had had to climb on to the capsule's roof at 2,400 m to undo the locks of the fuel tanks. When they had been released, the balloon stopped falling so fast. Ritchie's heroic act had probably saved their lives.

Out of control

On his second attempt, in Morocco in December 1997, Branson's balloon (worth £250,000 and one and a half times the height of Nelson's column in London – 51.85 m) flew off on its own while it was being filled with helium for take-off! The team watched in dismay as it set off towards the Atlas Mountains. All air-traffic controllers in the area had to be warned that this enormous balloon was flying, totally out of control, over their airspace.

The balloon landed in the foothills of the Atlas Mountains, just 30 miles (50 km) over the Algerian border. Negotiations were carried out with the Algerian authorities to get it back and the balloon was packed up and flown back to Morocco. Unfortunately, it was too damaged to be used again. Branson began to construct a new balloon for his next attempt.

Sheltered preparations

A sheltered place is usually used for inflating these enormous balloons to stop them being caught by the winds and blown away. American balloonists often use sports stadiums for this. *Breitling Orbiter 3* was inflated in a Swiss valley.

More flights

In 1997 and 1998 several other balloon teams had also taken off in an attempt to be the first round the world. Among them was Dick Rutan, now nearly 60, who had co-piloted *Voyager* (see page 80). However, Rutan did not achieve another world record. He and his crew had to bale out after their balloon got into difficulties not long after take-off.

Another ballooning team trying during this period were those on *Breitling Orbiter*, a balloon sponsored by a Swiss watch company, Breitling Watches. One of the members of the three-man team was Swiss man Bertrand Piccard, whose grandfather had set a record for height in a balloon in 1931, and whose father had set a record for depth in a submarine in the 1960s. Obviously a family of adventurers! But the *Orbiter* team had had their share of bad luck as well so far.

INTO 1999

At the end of 1998 and into 1999 the world watched as the balloon attempts kept coming. A combined flight with Branson,

Fossett and a Swede, Linderstrand, set off from Morocco on 18 December 1998 in *ICO Global*. This time they were *inside* the capsule when the balloon took off!

After flying across the Pacific in winds of up to 300 km/hr, changing weather conditions meant that they were unfortunately forced to ditch into the sea below them.

Airspace anxiety

Anyone wishing to fly over a country has to get permission from the aviation authorities in that country. Without this you can not enter a country's airspace.

In his December 1998 trip, Branson and his team annoyed the Chinese government by flying a different route over China (because of unexpected winds) from the one they had agreed. The Chinese government was furious at this change and ordered the balloon to land. Only the intervention of the British Prime Minister made the Chinese reluctantly agree to the balloon continuing over their country.

But the incident was going to have a bad effect on later ballooning attempts. The Chinese refused permission for any further British balloonists to fly over their country. This meant that some balloonists had to take even more fuel in order to fly round China. Attempting the round-the-world record was made even more difficult.

Will this one do it?

On 1 March 1999 the hot-air balloon, *Breitling Orbiter 3*, took off from a sheltered valley in the Swiss Alps, carrying Bertrand Piccard, 41, again and Brian Jones, British, 51. Both had considerable ballooning experience, but they knew that a strong rival was out in front of them – a hot-air balloon funded by Cable & Wireless was already in the air and doing well.

Breitling Orbiter 3 was bright silver in colour and 55 m high, as tall as a 20-storey building. It had been built by a British ballooning company at a cost of £2 million! Piccard and Jones were to live for the whole journey in a capsule which was only 5 m long and less then 3 m wide. There were bunks, a kitchen area, a heater and a toilet. Outside there were 28 gas cylinders.

Breitling Orbiter flies above the Swiss Alps soon after take-off.

THE JOURNEY BEGINS

4 March – *Orbiter* first travels south and then west to pick up the jet stream over north Africa. This takes the balloon east towards Libya. The temperature at the high altitude they are flying is –25°C and sometimes even colder. Large icicles – some as long as 1 m – start to form, slowing them down and wasting fuel. Piccard climbs out of the capsule to hack them off. It is a dangerous time for them all.

Inside the *Breitling Orbiter*. The tiny two-bed capsule where the two men spent three weeks.

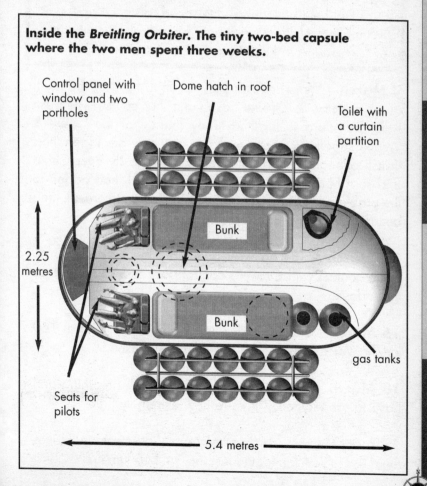

Control panel with window and two portholes

Dome hatch in roof

Toilet with a curtain partition

2.25 metres

Bunk

Bunk

gas tanks

Seats for pilots

5.4 metres

Jet Streams

Jet streams are motorways for balloonists! Jet streams are high fast-moving winds which occur where warm tropical air meets the cooler air north and south of the Tropics.

The winds here can be between 110–400 km/hr. They are at a height of 5½–8 miles (9–14 km) and can range in width from a few miles to thousands of miles. They help balloonists with speed, distance and duration. Modern passenger aircraft also use the jet streams to help them fly round the world.

7 March – Yemen refuses permission to fly over the north of the country, so *Orbiter* has to alter her course. The fresh food on board is finished. They learn that the Cable & Wireless balloon has ditched in the sea off Japan (this British expedition had not been allowed to fly over China and so it had had to carry more fuel, which had added to the problems). *Orbiter* is going to be allowed to cross China because it is not a British expedition

14 March – The halfway point! But there has been no radio contact with *Orbiter*'s control base in Switzerland for three days.

15 March – Strong winds carry the balloon along at 160 km/hr. Voice contact with base is re-established.

18 March – The crew have problems with breathing and have to use oxygen. They are now extremely tired.

19 March – They catch a favourable jet stream that takes them over the Atlantic, the last leg, at 145 km/hr.

The record-breaking route

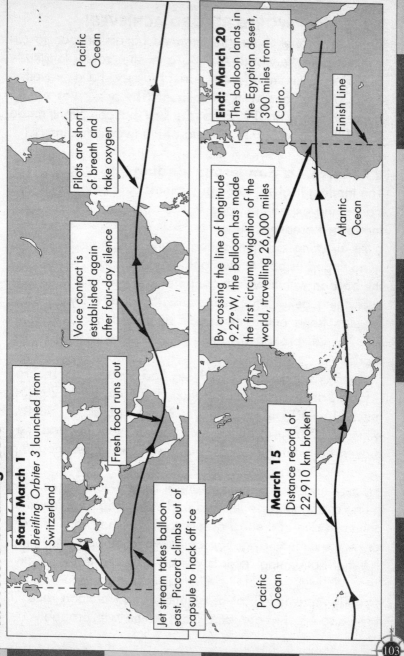

Start: March 1
Breitling Orbiter 3 launched from Switzerland

Jet stream takes balloon east. Piccard climbs out of capsule to hack off ice

Fresh food runs out

Voice contact is established again after four-day silence

Pilots are short of breath and take oxygen

Pacific Ocean

March 15
Distance record of 22,910 km broken

By crossing the line of longitude 9.27°W, the balloon has made the first circumnavigation of the world, travelling 26,000 miles

End: March 20
The balloon lands in the Egyptian desert, 300 miles from Cairo.

Finish Line

Atlantic Ocean

Pacific Ocean

20 March – WORLD RECORD ACHIEVED!

Breitling Orbiter is the first manned hot-air balloon to circumnavigate the world! At 9.45 a.m. she crosses longitude 9.27°W (over north-west Africa). They have travelled 26,000 miles and won $1 million! (The prize was put up by a company in 1997 for the first balloon flight made round the world before the end of the twentieth century.)

21 March – a dangerous landing

The landing is always one of the most dangerous parts of a ballooning expedition, and it was no easy touch-down for the record breakers.

As *Breitling Orbiter* landed in the Egyptian desert, the wind tipped its basket over and the crew had to run around the balloon with knives, tearing holes in the material to stop everything being dragged across the desert. They waited for eight hours before they could be picked up and taken to join the celebrations of their ground crew ... and of the world.

The FAI (see page 12) said they had broken three records – for distance, time and duration. They had flown 29,056 miles (46,760 km) in 19 days, 21 hours and 55 minutes, often at 10,600 m above the ground. Not only had they broken ballooning records, but it was the longest non-stop aerial flight in history!

Jones and Piccard had endured three weeks together in a tiny cramped capsule, cold and exhausted. But they had achieved one of the last great records of the twentieth century – the circumnavigation of the world by balloon.

What ballooning records will be achieved in the twenty-first century? A solo circumnavigation of the world? Already there is talk of a round-the-world balloon race. If this happens, Piccard and Jones's time will probably be broken, but no one else can take away their achievement. No one else can ever be first to go round the world in a balloon now!

A WALK ROUND
THE WORLD

How *do* you walk round the world? You might well ask! Well, the *Guinness Book of Records* says that a walk round the world must include the following:

- The walk must start and finish in the same place
- You must cross four continents

You probably won't be surprised to hear that not many people have tried to walk round the world. An expedition like this needs a great deal of time, energy and determination – not to mention the ability to put up with some very bad blisters!

An early walker
The first person who was supposed to have walked round the world was an American, George Schilling. He is said to have carried out his walk between 1887 and 1904.

THE FIRST RECORD MAKER
The first-ever *verified* walk round the world was made by

David Kunst, also an American, who walked 14,450 miles (23,250 km) across four continents from 20 June 1970 to 5 October 1974.

Kunst started with his brother, John, from their home town in Minnesota, USA, and walked east to the Atlantic coast, with a mule to carry their belongings. After crossing to Portugal, they walked across to Bulgaria, again with a mule towing a wagon in which they slept at nights. Next it was Turkey and Iran, and into Afghanistan.

But here something terrible happened ...

Bandit attack

The brothers were walking with their mule in empty, lonely mountains, miles from any towns or other human beings. It was a moonlit night. They stopped and went to sleep in a gorge.

Suddenly David awoke to find shadowy figures moving in on them. He fired his gun. The sound echoed around the gorge. There was silence and the figures melted back into the night.

The brothers breathed a sigh of relief. But then one of the bandits fired a shot.

'Run!' John yelled.

They turned and ran towards the wagon to try and get some sort of cover from the attack. David fell. He'd been shot in the chest ...

'Play dead!' he yelled to his brother.

David felt someone grab him and turn him over roughly as his watch was taken off. He let his left hand fall heavily as if he were a dead man. He could hear the bandits going through the stuff on the wagon. He later discovered that the attackers were look-ing for the large amount of money they believed the American brothers were carrying. They had heard that the walkers were raising money for a charity but they didn't realize that the Kunsts were asking people to send the money to the charity itself. The bandits thought people were giving it to the brothers.

Eventually David heard the sound of a truck approaching. There were voices, commands, a slamming door and then the truck drove off fast.

David was in great pain from his gunshot wound. Every breath felt as though he was being stabbed in the chest. He turned his head slowly and looked round. About 3 m away lay John, totally still. Was he also playing dead? Or was he *really* dead?

David crawled towards John over the rough ground and turned him over. A horrifying sight met his eyes. John had been shot in the head. The bandits had killed his brother.

Setting out again

David eventually got a lift in a passing truck back to Kabul, the capital of Afghanistan. Here his serious wounds were nursed in a hospital. Then he flew home.

People expected him to stop this crazy round-the-world walk now, but he was determined to continue with it for his brother's sake. He felt he owed it to John to complete it.

So David returned to Afghanistan, to the spot where John had been killed, and set out again. His other brother, Pete, joined him for a year. They walked on across Afghanistan, into Pakistan and down through India.

In Australia the desert flies were unbearable. Pete left in central Australia. His year was up and he was returning to his family. But David continued. He eventually reached Sydney.

The homeward trek

The final part of Kunst's walk was from the Pacific coast of America towards his home town. He often got terribly dehydrated because he wasn't carrying enough water. He was walking on his own, with a small backpack. It was to prove very tough in the American desert, with no way of taking extra water and no shelter for the night. Deserts often get very hot during the day but they can be very cold when the sun goes down.

One freezing-cold desert night he found himself near a filling station. He slept in the tiny gents toilet, where he kept pushing the hand dryer again and again until he got the room warm enough to sleep in!

EXTREME FACTS
DEHYDRATION

Dehydration happens when your body does not get enough water. As the human body is made up of about two-thirds water it is very important to take in plenty of liquid. An adult needs to drink at least 2.5–3 litres of water or other liquids a day. But walking in the heat of the desert makes you sweat and water is lost very quickly from the body, along with salt. You then need to drink more, especially fluids that contain sugars and salts, to replace what you have lost.

If you are becoming dehydrated you will start to feel thirsty, weak and tired. If you still don't drink anything, things get more serious:

- You will get confused and be unable to concentrate
- Your mouth and tongue will feel very dry
- Your eyes will look sunken
- Your pulse will get weak

On 5 October 1974, Kunst reached his home town. His brother Pete joined him for the last part of the journey, saying that two Kunst brothers had started on this epic trek and so two would finish. Yes, David Kunst had walked round the world, but it had been a tragic triumph.

> Kunst wore out 22 pairs of shoes on his trek round the world!

OTHER RECORD BREAKERS

A faster, later walking record is held by another American. Steven Newman walked round the world from 1 April 1983 to 1 April 1987. He covered 15,509 miles (24,959 km), visiting 20 countries.

And yet another American, Arthur Blessitt, is a world walker too! Blessit started walking on 25 December 1969 and has walked 32,002 miles (51,500 km) since then. He has been to 267 countries, preaching as he walked and pulling a 3.5 m high cross.

And has a woman walked round the world? Read on for the story of Ffyona Campbell.

Walking the world!

On 14 October 1994 British woman Ffyona Campbell entered into the record books when she walked to the sign post at John O'Groats at the top of Scotland. She claimed to be the third person ever to have walked round the world – and the first woman. This journey, done in different stages, had taken over 11 years. She began at the age of 16 and covered a mammoth 20,000 miles (32,000 km).

But, later, in 1996 Campbell admitted that she hadn't walked the entire way. On the 3,000 mile (4,800 km) American part of her journey (in 1985) she had hitched a lift in her backup vehicle for 1,000 miles (1,600 km). She used to get out at the edge of a town and walk in to the press conference, claiming she had walked the whole way from the last stop. She had taken the lifts because she had not been feeling well and found the 25 miles

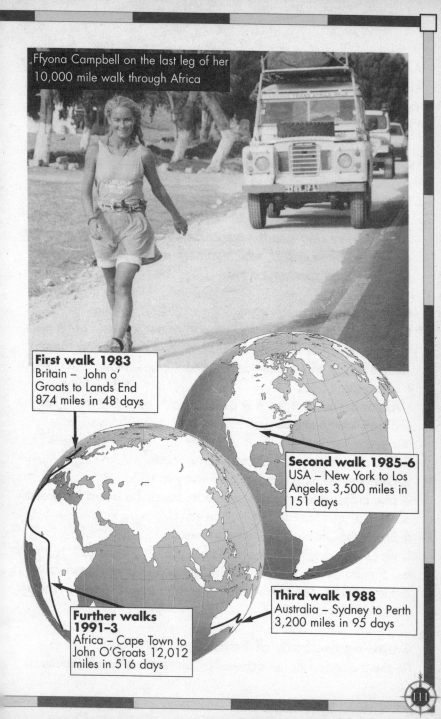

Ffyona Campbell on the last leg of her 10,000 mile walk through Africa

First walk 1983
Britain – John o' Groats to Lands End 874 miles in 48 days

Second walk 1985–6
USA – New York to Los Angeles 3,500 miles in 151 days

Third walk 1988
Australia – Sydney to Perth 3,200 miles in 95 days

Further walks 1991–3
Africa – Cape Town to John O'Groats 12,012 miles in 516 days

(40 km) a day she had been planning to walk too much.

After this she walked the whole way across Australia, then up Africa, and finally across Europe to Britain and, ultimately, back up to John O'Groats, where she'd first set out from in 1983.

In October 1994 she was applauded in the media and elsewhere with great excitement. However, when she admitted that she had cheated, she said she hadn't been able to live with her lie. She wrote,

'Once you've lied about your achievements, you've created a burden for yourself, which you can never, never put down. My lie almost destroyed me.'

Global feat?

Campbell may have cheated on part of her journey, but it must be admitted that to walk 20,000 miles (32,000 km) through such a range of terrain – desert, bush, cities, mountains – was an incredible feat.

Campbell got her first key pieces of advice from John Hillaby, a British long-distance walker:

1 Decide where you will begin and end.
2 Get a good map (Ordnance Survey in UK).
3 Use cross-country routes, not main roads (to avoid the worst of the traffic).
4 Break the distance down into weeks.
5 Have one day off in six (something to look forward to).
6 25 miles (40 km) a day is OK, but build up to it gradually.
7 Never think about the whole journey; take it one day at a time.

Breaking the back of Britain

As she got ready for her first walk, Campbell's only intention was to go from the top to the bottom of Britain. She trained for this walk by putting telephone directories into her rucksack and walking laps round Hyde Park in London.

On 16 August 1983 Campbell dipped her toe in the North Sea at the top of Scotland. Then she turned south. She knew that she had about 50 days of walking in front of her.

Aches and pains

On the first day she walked for 5 hours and 26 minutes, much of it in the rain. She was feeling quite pleased with herself. However, when she woke up on day two her muscles were aching so much she could hardly move! Yet, she knew that she had to get out of bed because a journalist from a newspaper was there to report on her journey. She would be so humiliated if she gave up after just one day!

By day six she had a bad knee, but she continued on. As the days went by, she found that she was actually beginning to enjoy the walking because she felt she was proving something to herself. At the end of each day she would mark the road with a piece of chalk, and started again from this point the following morning. This was to become a tradition for all her future walks.

She was almost sad as she approached Land's End almost 50 days later. Her sister was there to meet her and sprayed her with champagne. Campbell had also raised £25,000 for a London cancer hospital – this she felt *was* an achievement.

At this stage she still had no intention of walking round the world, but ...

Across America

After some jobs and some travelling, Campbell decided she wanted to walk across America. She wrote, phoned and faxed, but had little success at getting sponsors. She decided to set out from New York in June

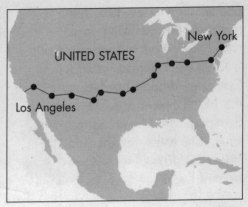

1985 and aim to reach Los Angeles, on the west coast, in December – so she would be walking across the American desert in winter. She had reckoned that 6 days a week at 25 miles (40 km) a day would take her about 6 months.

Campbell started her walk in the traffic fumes of New York City. Her two-man backup team drove a camper van which they were all going to stay in overnight. As she walked across Pennsylvania, the July heat was very humid. She walked on until she had covered 1,000 miles (1,600 km), more than her British walk. It was here that she began to cheat, taking lifts in her backup van.

In the desert she started walking all day again. The days were very cold, seldom above zero. At night, as she slept in the camper van, the temperature dropped as low as –10°C.

She made her way on to Los Angeles, which she reached in January 1986. She walked down to the beach, took off her shoes and walked in to the sea – she had reached the Pacific Ocean! But she was very disappointed that none of the news-papers or TV people had taken any interest in her achievement.

The Australian trek

Next Campbell decided to walk across Australia. She set out from the Pacific Ocean, which rolled on to Bondi Beach, Sydney. She was aiming for the Indian Ocean, on the other side of Australia.

She walked through Sydney and out on the road towards Canberra, the capital city. Much of this part of the journey was on a main highway. Big long-haul trucks whizzed passed her. It was very unpleasant.

As in America, she was dependent on a backup driver for food and water – only one person this time. He had a tough job too – driving ahead to set up press contacts, racing back to meet Campbell and to feed and water her at several points, then driving on again to set up the camper van for the night.

Campbell walked 40 miles (64 km) a day in the first week. She had a break every two and a half hours, which meant that she spent 15 hours altogether on the road (actual walking time was about 12 hours). She often had to give a press interview at the end of it all when she was tired. Then she had to carry out stretching exercises to try and stop her muscles stiffening before the next day.

But she had planned to put the mileage up to 50 miles (80 km) a day after the first week. Could she do this? She followed the advice that Hillaby (see page 112) had given her all those years before – break the distance down into manageable bits. She persevered and made it to Melbourne ...

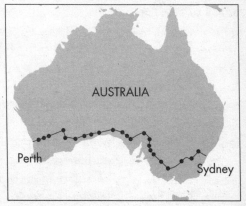

Big blisters!

… but not without problems. One evening, when she took her shoes and socks off to examine a sore patch that had been bothering her during the day's walk, she found that she had a bad blister. Her support driver syringed the fluid out of it. He'd persuaded her that this was the best way to treat it.

Over the next day Campbell continued walking, though her foot got sorer and sorer. That was hardly surprising. The blister had grown during the day and had turned into two sections. It now throbbed terribly.

At every break, when Campbell met up with her driver, David, he not only gave her food and water, but he also re-syringed the blisters, filled them with more antiseptic and then dressed them again. Despite this, the blisters didn't get better, but worse. And still new ones appeared. Campbell continued on her way. Later she wrote:

Over the thousands of miles which followed, David pulled pints of pus out of my feet every week. There were blisters within blisters, overlayers of blisters, blisters with … infections, and blisters deep under calluses, around my heels and between toes. But mostly they spread across the soles of my feet.

EXTREME FACTS
BLISTERS

Blisters are bubbles filled with liquid that appear on the skin. One cause of them is continuous rubbing in one place, which is why they often appear on the feet. There are two theories on how to treat blisters:

1 Leave them alone!

2 a. Pick with a sterile needle (put in a flame first)

> **b**. Carefully take off the excess skin
> **c**. Wash with salted water
> **d**. Put on an anti-bacterial dressing
> **e**. Cover with a dry dressing (and perhaps a bandage to cushion and prevent further damage)

Campbell walked across the Eyre Peninsula and on to the desert, where the temperature rose to 60°C. It was so hot that the soles of her shoes stuck to the melting surface of the road. She tried to breathe in short little puffs, because she was afraid that the hot, hot air would burn her lungs. But this short breathing gave her nose bleeds. She also had to cover up her head and face to keep the flies off. She found she was getting dehydrated very quickly.

The heat was so unbearable that she decided to walk at night to try and avoid the worst of it. Eventually she reached Perth and the Indian Ocean, 3,200 miles (5,150 km) and 95 days after she had started in Sydney.

This was the halfway point in a walking journey round the world.

African adventures

The *Guinness Book of Records* states that four continents need to be crossed to achieve a walking record. Campbell decided to cross Africa rather than Asia – one reason being that it was difficult to get more than a 24-hour visa for Iran.

Visas

If you are travelling through the different countries of the world, you will usually need to get permission to enter in the form of a visa – a stamp on your passport (and perhaps a piece of paper too) from that country's authority. How hard it is to get a visa often depends on your nationality.

Preparing to walk across Africa was very different from her previous trips. There was a lot more to do. Campbell needed to arrange visas for the different countries she was planning to cross, organize injections against diseases, and sort out a suitable back-up vehicle (a camper van would certainly not do this time; she needed a four-wheel drive vehicle for the bad

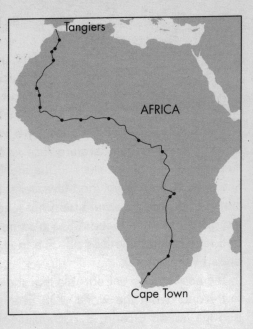

roads and rough ground, with a spare of practically everything). Then she had to consider food and water – and even the need to learn a few words of the local languages.

Setting out

Again she started off by walking out of the sea, this time the Southern Ocean at Cape Town, and set off northwards with the aim of crossing the whole continent of Africa. It was to be her hardest trek yet.

She walked through South Africa and into Botswana and across the Kalahari Desert. The Landrover found the desert difficult going and had to be dug out on several occasions.

Then she was in Zambia. A pattern had now been established: the drivers waited with the Landrover 10 miles (16 km) ahead of her. The walk had been tough so far, but it was going well.

That is until she encountered the tsetse flies ...

EXTREME FACTS
THE TSETSE FLY

This is a vampire fly! These horrible little insects fly in large swarms, sometimes a mile wide, and suck out blood from their victims. Tsetse flies even pierce the thick skin of a hippopotamus. They can cause a nasty sleeping sickness in humans and cattle.

The walk that day was horrendous. Campbell was continuously surrounded by an enormous swarm of the flies and had to cover herself from head to toe. She wore a hat with a mosquito net covering it, long sleeves, long trousers, and tucked the ends of her trousers into her socks. She pulled down her sleeves, hanging on to the ends with her clenched fists to stop her hands being bitten.

She lashed out at the flies but they kept buzzing around. One got under the mosquito net ... another sneaked under her ankle grips, went up her leg and injected her thigh with its poison. Others managed to find ways of attacking her elsewhere. It was horrific. As the heat of midday approached, the flies got nastier and nastier. Her right eye had now swollen up from a bite and was closing rapidly.

Something bigger ...
But another, potentially even more dangerous, problem now arose. An old fisherman she passed told her that a lion had been spotted in the area. It was a lone male, usually the most dangerous. Campbell's fear was great as she walked alone with the tsetse flies still swarming about her. She constantly checked over her shoulder and all around her for the prowling lion.

But things got even worse! The African continent seemed to throw several of its greatest difficulties at her in one day.

Bush fires

She turned a corner and found bush fires in front of her. The dry grass on either side of the track was burning and flames of yellow leaped across her trail. The track itself was burning too in some places.

How did the backup Landrover get through all this? she thought. Maybe the fire had started afterwards and the Landrover couldn't get back to rescue her. What could she do?

She had little choice. She found herself running and jumping – again and again – over the clumps of flame, still with some of the tsetse flies buzzing around her. But she did eventually reach the Land Rover. She was exhausted, bitten, swollen from the many bites, and her right eye was shut. But she was safe!

Later they discovered that the flies in this area were so bad that only four people lived there!

Could worse things happen to her on this trip? Well, yes they could ...

Campbell continued on towards the Zaire border, walking through villages. In one, soldiers (who thought she might perhaps be a spy because there was a war going on in Zaire) arrested her. The Landrover team was also arrested. They were all held for two days.

War zones

It was the war in Zaire that finally put a stop to Campbell's walk. The danger from this was too great and she and her team were advised to leave.

But this woman was not to be put off. Six months later she was back in Africa. She now walked west to avoid the various wars and so went through Nigeria and then on through Mali and out across the Sahara Desert.

Mine fields

Part of this desert walk was through a large mine field – 400 hundred miles (640 km) of danger, in fact. They had guides for parts of the journey, but at one point Campbell had to walk in front of the Landrover to keep a look-out for anti-tank mines. Her own weight wouldn't set them off, but it would be a different matter if the Landrover went over the top of one. It was a relief to reach the Moroccan border.

Campbell kept on walking until she stepped into the Mediterranean Sea, at Tangiers.

Europe

Eight months later Campbell was walking again, this time on her homeward journey across Europe. She started on the beach in southern Spain and set out for Calais in northern France. It was 30 April 1994.

She wanted to be alone on this trip, so she had no back-up team and walked with just a rucksack, camping at night.

Then at last she was back in England, in Dover, on the coast opposite Calais! Here young people from the adventure charity, Raleigh International, joined her as she walked north towards John O'Groats.

On 14 October 1994 she reached her target, and put her feet into the North Atlantic Ocean! She had great coverage in the press, everyone congratulating her on being the first woman to walk round the world.

Confession

After Campbell confessed to cheating in America, her name

was taken out of the record books. However, she did later go back to walk the 1,000 mile (1,600 km) stretch she had missed in America and so, eventually, did walk around the entire world. She has now satisfied the *Guiness Book of Records* criteria.

Tough going
Walking the world is tough going – for anyone, woman or man – as Campbell's experiences prove. Could you put up with all those difficulties and still keep going?

CONQUERING
EXTREME EXPEDITIONS
THE WORLD

MAKING NEW
RECORDS

'MAD BUT MARVELLOUS!'

'Mad but marvellous!' are the words that HRH Prince Charles used to describe the first overland round-the-world expedition via the poles – the Transglobe Expedition. It was an amazing journey, one that the British leader, Sir Ranulph Fiennes, and his team on many occasions thought that they might never achieve.

But achieve it they did! In August 1982 Sir Ranulph Fiennes and Charlie Burton arrived back in London having been around the entire world overland via its polar axis. They had travelled south through Europe, then across the Sahara desert, followed by a sea voyage along the coast of west Africa and down to Antarctica, over this vast continent via the South Pole, north across the Pacific, up the Yukon River in Canada, and then across practically uninhabited land to the very edge of the Arctic Ocean! Finally they travelled over this ocean via the North Pole and back down to London.

Planning ahead

They couldn't have done any of this without a lot of help – the expedition took a whole seven years of planning. Fiennes drew together an enormous number of supporters, including Prince Charles who became the expedition's patron. Fiennes' wife, Ginny, was one of his hardest co-workers (in fact, the expedition had been her idea!). Everything for the expedition was given free or paid for by sponsors, which took an enormous amount of organization. When one man, Anton Bowring, offered his services free as a member of the expedition ship crew, Fiennes said, 'Great! But we need to find a ship first! Can you get us one?' And he did!

The *Benjamin Bowring* was a 30-year-old ice strengthened vessel and was sponsored by both a British and an American insurance company. It was this ship that carried Fiennes and Burton from Africa down to Antarctica and then, one year later, from the other side of Antarctica up the Pacific to the Yukon River. Finally (another year later!) it took them home to London from the other side of the Arctic Ocean.

Planning the 100,000 mile route the adventurers took depended on two very important factors:

● it was only possible to cross via the poles during their short summers
● the journey to reach the Arctic Ocean by small open boat through the north Canadian islands (via the North-west Passage) could only be attempted when the sea ice had begun to break up (but it had to be completed before it froze over again!).

The whole trip had to be arranged around these climatic considerations.

Perils of the poles
For Fiennes and Burton the toughest parts of the trip were travelling through the two freezing polar regions. In Antarctica they

spent the winter months on the edge of the continent so they would be able to set off as soon as the warmer weather came. They travelled (here together with Ollie Shepard), mainly on Skidoos pulling sledges with their rations and equipment on board. They were also supplied by aeroplane drops. The men had many frightening and dangerous moments in Antarctica, especially when encountering deep crevasses and whiteouts. However, despite the dangers, they managed to explore and map a huge area of the continent where no human had ever been before.

In the Arctic they had an even more perilous time – for example, just getting their motorized rubber dinghies into the mouth of the Yukon River proved a life-threatening experience when one capsized; then, once on the river itself, they were faced with some extremely hazardous canyons full of wild waves.

The men overwintered on the edge of the Arctic Ocean and set out as soon as they could on skis or snow-shoes (as conditions demanded) pulling their sledges. They had to be swift as, the warmer the weather got, the more likely it was that the sea ice would melt and crack apart. This would make their crossing attempt impossible.

But even that year's quicker-than-normal melting ice failed to halt the Transglobe Expedition and these extreme explorers reached the North Pole, crossed the rest of the Arctic Ocean (including three months floating on an enormous ice floe that was often investigated by frightening polar bears!) to arrive back in London nearly three years after they had started on their epic adventure.

There was great excitement – as well as being the first people to circumnavigate the world on its polar axis, they were the also the first humans ever to reach both poles overland! An extraordinary expedition and one of the last great achievements of the 20th century.

FASTER AND FASTER

By aeroplane
The fastest air circumnavigation of the globe was made in 1995 by an Air France Concorde (with refuelling stops). It flew from New York to New York via France, the Middle East, Thailand, Guam (a Pacific island), Honolulu and Mexico. The time was 32 hours, 22 minutes and 49 seconds.

By space rocket
The first human to go round the world in a space rocket was Soviet cosmonaut Yuri Gagarin. He completed a single orbit of the earth in 1961, going round the world in just 1 hour and 48 minutes. Talk about conquering the globe!

By motorized boat
The fastest trip by a motorized boat has been by the *Cable & Wireless Adventurer*, which circled the world in 74 days, 9 hours and 54 minutes in 1998, to and from Gibraltar. The American nuclear submarine, USS *Triton*, had set the previous record at 83 days. *Adventurer*'s crew was aiming to beat not only this record but also the fictional Phileas Fogg's record of 80 days (see page 13). They achieved both!

By scheduled flights
How long do you think it would take to go round the world by flying on regular airlines? Well, sticking to FAI regulations (see page 12), in 1980, British man David Springbett covered 23,068 miles (37,123 km) in just 44 hours and 6 minutes. He flew to and from Los Angeles via London, Bahrain, Singapore, Bangkok, Manila, Tokyo and Honolulu. This sort of journey would take a lot of studying of airline routes and timetables!

By car

The first circumnavigation of the world by car was by an Indian husband and wife team, Mohammed and Neena Choudhury from Calcutta, in 1989. They drove more than an Equator's length (or 24,901.41 road miles/40,074 km) round the world – putting them in the *Guinness Book of Records*.

Speeding tickets
The *Guinness Book of Records* says that if you get booked for speeding, in any country, while trying to drive round the world, you are disqualified!

By land vehicle

In December 1997 a British team returned to London after motoring their way round the world via its antipodal points (ie: points on opposite sides of the world) in 21 days, 2 hours and 14 minutes of driving time – free of speeding tickets! This beat the previous record of this type by 18 days. The three-man team had covered 18,344 miles (29,521 km).

They encountered torrential rain and floods in Pakistan, heat of 50°C in Australia (not to mention a night-time collision with a kangaroo), and ice and snow in Alaska. But despite all their difficulties their four-wheel drive car didn't break down!

By helicopter

In 1996 two Americans flew westwards round the world by helicopter in 17 days, 6 hours and 25 seconds, from London and back.

By motorbike

In 1997 British man Nick Saunders circumnavigated the globe on a motorbike, in a *Guinness Book of Records* time of 31 days and 20 hours, between 18 April and 9 June.

OTHER ADVENTURERS

By wheelchair
Rick Hansen (Canadian), who had been paralysed from the waist down after a car accident, wheeled his wheelchair through 34 countries in 4 continents – a distance of nearly 25,000 miles (40,000 km) from 21 March 1985 to 22 May 1987.

Cycling
Many people have set out to cycle round the world. Some aim to do it as fast as possible, while others want to see as much as possible.

Tal Burt, from Israel, is in the *Guinness Book of Records* for being the fastest. He cycled round the world in 77 days, 14 hours in 1992, covering 13,329 road miles or 21,450 km!

In the 1970s a British couple travelled round the world on a tandem bicycle, covering 18,020 miles (29,000 km) in 18 months.

Others, from teenagers to grandparents, cycle round the world for various reasons. Anne Mustoe, a retired British headmistress in her fifties, wanted to do something different and see the world. Rob Penn, a London solicitor in his twenties, wanted adventure.

Checklist for cyclists according to Rob Penn

Ten things you should never be without when cycling round the world:
- A short-wave radio
- Frisbee (useful in the camp kitchen as a dish and a great way to make friends on the beach)
- Internationally accepted credit card for financial emergencies
- Spare camera batteries
- Sunglasses and strings to attach sunglasses to your head
- Camera tripod
- Bottle of tea-tree oil
- Roll of surgical tape to cover insect bites
- Family photographs
- Portable water filter

AROUND THE EQUATOR

At the end of the nineteenth century a writer called Mark Twain travelled round the world following the Equator and wrote about his experiences. In the late twentieth century another writer, Peter Ustinov, followed Twain's journey and published a book about it. People find it interesting to compare journeys today with past ones to see what has changed — even the ones that never happened ...

Around the world in 80 days

Phileas Fogg's unreal record (see page 13) is still a challenge for people who want to see if they can get round the world in less than 80 days using only transport that would have been available to Fogg – i.e. no aeroplanes or fast ocean-going yachts!

In 1984 British journalist Nicholas Coleridge managed to get round with 38 hours and 10 minutes to spare, using trains, steamers, taxis and even an elephant and a camel!

In 1988 British television presenter Michael Palin set off with a BBC TV crew to make a global journey following in Fogg's footsteps. Modern technology now lets us sit back and watch what happens to people like Palin! This is what we call armchair travelling.

Michael Palin followed the original journey faithfully, leaving from the same starting point, the Reform Club in London, to try to get round the entire world in fewer than 80 days. In 1873, when Fogg was supposed to have made this epic trip, it was difficult enough. But Michael Palin found it even harder going in modern times!

● In Victorian times, there were no airlines and people usually travelled abroad by sea, so there were lots of passenger ships around. These days it is a different matter. If you're not allowed to fly, it isn't easy to travel long distances. Most of Palin's longer journeys had to be made by cargo ship – not very comfortable, especially when there are no cabins and you have to sleep on deck!

● In 1873 the British Empire was very powerful and if you were British it wasn't too tricky to get permission to enter countries all over the world. But Michael Palin found it very different for the modern-day adventurer. He was often delayed due to the problems of getting visas to enter various countries.

Palin nearly didn't make it. On the final panic-stricken stretch, a delay on the London Underground (due to a suspicious package) caused a few nail-biting moments. But luckily the train eventually moved on and he made it back to the Reform Club in the nick of time! He had taken 79 days and 7 hours to make the global journey, in which he had travelled by ship, train, taxi and even by balloon and camel.

IN A DIFFERENT WAY

A family at sea

A British couple who wanted to give their three children real-life geography lessons set off in a 13-m yacht, *Maamari*, in September 1997 to sail round the world. The youngest child was a two-week-old baby and the other two were aged four and five.

Mr Schinas said he and his wife had no plans to return to Britain. They just wanted to sail wherever the mood took them. He continued: 'My children have never watched television, used a computer or eaten a Big Mac. Their education is travelling with us, watching dolphins swim beside the hull.'

By horse-drawn caravan

How about this for a way to break a record? Travelling round the world for seven years in a horse-drawn caravan!

A Scottish family, the Grants, decided that they were bored with normal life and so they sold their house in Scotland in 1990 and set off round the world! The children were then 10, 9 and 7. They travelled across 3 continents and 15 countries. The children studied along the way and also spent two terms in a school in Slovenia.

Disaster on a bottle raft

In 1984 a couple who were trying to sail round the world on a raft made of driftwood and plastic bottles were shipwrecked just 70 miles (110 km) after they had left their starting point of

Southampton in England. They said they were determined to try again!

On your skates

In March 1996 Frenchman Fabrice Gropaiz set out to roller-skate round the world! He skated across America, and then across Europe from France to Russia. He had to stop in Russia because the roads were frozen and no good for skating at that time of year. But he returned later, in 1998, to continue his skate. Where is he now? Will he be the first to roller skate round the world?

Keep an eye on the newspapers to see what records people are attempting next!

Checklist for a round-the-world trip

As you'll have discovered from these stories, a global adventurer needs to do a lot of planning and organization before going on their journey of a lifetime. Here are the most important things to remember before leaving:

- [ ] How will you travel? Look at a map and plan your journey well.
- [ ] Plan regular breaks. You'll be glad to have something to look forward to – you'll need them!
- [ ] Work out what you will do about food and drink – this is very important!
- [ ] What health preparations do you need for your type of journey? Do you need to get fit? What about injections against diseases? What do you need in your medical kit? Much of this will depend on the countries you are visiting.
- [ ] What will the climate and weather be like? Be prepared and take the right clothes.

- [ ] What special equipment do you need, i.e. water filter, tents?
- [ ] Do you need permission or visas to enter the countries you plan to visit?
- [ ] Will you travel alone or with someone else? If so, who? Will you get on with them on a long trip or if a crisis occurs?
- [ ] Will you take any luxuries like special food or a perhaps a Frisbee or a football?
- [ ] Do you need to learn any important words in other languages? Will you need a phrase book?
- [ ] Talk to as many experts and people who have already done this kind of trip as possible. They will give you lots of tips and advice from their own experiences .

And finally ...

Many people are setting out to go round the world nowadays, some to break records, others just for the fun and the experience. They all have great adventures. To travel round the world – in any way – is an amazing experience that our ancestors could never have imagined doing.

Not all the round-the-world achievements in this book are officially recognized in *The Guiness Book of Records*. But every single one of the individuals who took part in the adventures described here has shown an enormous amount of courage and determination, whether or not they were the first to do something or to break an existing record.

Can you think of a new or different way to go round the world? Would you aim to be the fastest, or would you try to see as many different places as possible and to meet as many people from different cultures as possible? Do you think that *you* could end up breaking a record one day?

TIMELINE

1519–22   First circumnavigation of the world. The *Vittoria* returns to Spain after a three-year voyage, led by Ferdinand Magellan (he was killed during the voyage, but the ship completed the voyage under the command of d'Elcano).

1577–80   Englishman, Sir Francis Drake, leads the first voyage with the aim of circumnavigating the world. The *Golden Hind* is the only one of his five ships to complete the journey.

Over the next two hundred years other voyages circumnavigate the world in their search for trade routes and new territories (often with the loss of ships and always with the loss of many sailors' lives). Two of the most significant of these expeditions are led by Englishman, Captain James Cook between 1768–1775. His scientists and artists record much information about the Pacific Islands and Australia, as well as the icy waters of the Antarctic Ocean.

1764   When a French ship, *La Boudeuse*, reaches port, it is discovered that one of the servants on board is a woman who is disguised as a man. She is probably the first woman to travel around the world.

1876–77   A rich British man, Sir Thomas Brassey, circumnavigates the world in style in a sailing ship called *Sunbeam*, together with his wife and family, servants, a doctor, three cooks, and a crew of 22.

1895–98   Captain Joshua Slocum (American), in his yacht *Spray*, is the first person to sail solo around the world.

1887–1904 American George Schilling is probably the first person to walk around the world.

1924   The first air journey around the world is completed in 69 stages by two US Army Air Service open cockpit single engine biplanes.

1924   The German airship the *Graf Zeppelin* circumnavigates the world in 21 days.

1933   American Wiley Post is the first person to fly solo around the world.

1949   A US Air Force B-50 is the first aircraft to fly around the world without landing. The aeroplane is refuelled in flight and the time is 93 hours.

1961   Yuri Gagarin (Soviet) is the first human to go around the world in a space rocket.

1964   American Jerrie Mock is the first woman to fly solo around the world.

1966–67   Sir Francis Chichester (British) sails alone around the world in *Gipsy Moth*, with only one stop-over in Sydney, Australia.

1968–69   Sir Robin Knox-Johnston (British) is the first person to sail alone and non-stop around the world according to the *Guinness Book of Records* rules (see page 12). His yacht is called *Suhaili* and the voyage takes 313 days.

1970–71   Chay Blyth (British), is the first person to sail, alone and non-stop, westwards (against the winds of the Southern Ocean) around the world. The voyage takes 293 days.

1970–74   American David Kunst is the first person who is verified by the *Guinness Book of Records* as having walked around the world.

1978   The year in which three different yachtswoman complete single-handed circumnavigations of the world via various routes – Krystyna Chojnowska-Liskiewwicz (Polish), Naomi James (British), and Brigitte Oudry (French).

1979–82   British men Sir Ranuph Fiennes and Charlie Burton, on the Transglobe Expedition, are the first men to go around the world overland following its polar axis (ie via the poles).

1986   Americans Dick Rutan and Jeana Yeager fly the specially designed aircraft *Voyager* around the world in nine days without refuelling.

1983–87   American Steven Newman sets the fastest record to date for walking around the world, 1st April 1983–1 April 1987.

1984–87   Australian Serge Testa sails around the world in the smallest boat ever – just 3.5 m long!

1985–87   Canadian Rick Hansen is the first person to go around the world in a wheelchair. He covers a distance of nearly 25,000 miles over four continents.

1987–88   Australian Kay Cottee is the first woman to sail around the world solo and non-stop. The voyage takes 189 days in her yacht *Blackmore's First Lady*.

1990   The first all female crewed yacht sails around the world – *Maiden*, captained by British woman Tracy Edwards in the Whitbread race.

1992   Tal Burt, from Israel, is the fastest man to cycle around the world to date. He covers over 13,000 miles in 77 days.

1993   French yachtsman Bruno Peyron and his crew are the first people to win the Jules Verne Trophy – for sailing around the world in fewer than 80 days. They take 79 days, 6 hours, 15 minutes and 56 seconds.

1994   Mike Golding (British) sets new record of 161 days for sailing westwards around the world.

1994   Ffyona Campbell (British) claims to be the first woman to walk around the world.

1995   Concorde makes the fastest air circumnavigation of the globe to date (with refuelling stops) – in 32 hours, 22 minutes and 49 seconds.

1997   Olivier de Kersauson (French) and crew, set a new record of 71 days, 14 hours, 22 minutes and 8 seconds for sailing around the world.

1997   The Grant family (from Scotland) complete a seven-year round the world journey by horse-drawn caravan.

1998   British man Brian Milton is the first person to fly around the world in a microlight.

1999   The hot air balloon *Breitling Orbiter*, piloted by Bertrand Piccard (Swiss) and Brian Jones (British), is the first to circumnavigate the world. The time is 19 days, 21 hours and 55 minutes.

GLOSSARY

Aerial
Describes something that happens or operates in the air.

Autopilot
Short for automatic pilot. A device for keeping an aircraft or boat on a set course.

Aviator
Another word for a pilot.

Barren
Land that can't grow trees or plants.

Blizzard
A very severe snow storm with strong winds.

Calorie
A unit of energy. Usually used to measure the energy contained in food.

Cape
A headland, or piece of land that juts out from the mainland.

Capsize
When a boat capsizes, she turns on her side in the water.

Cargo
Goods carried on a ship, aircraft, or motor vehicle.

Circumnavigate
Circum means 'around' in Latin, so circumnavigate means to find our way round something (see **Navigate**). A circumnavigation is usually taken to mean a round-the-world journey.

Climate
The usual weather conditions in a particular area.

Cockpit
Where the pilot(s) sits in an aircraft.

Compass
An instrument containing a magnetized pointer which shows the direction of magnetic north. It is used to navigate (see **Navigate**).

Convoy
A group of ships or vehicles travelling together.

Culmination
The highest point of something.

Current
A body of water (or air) moving in a definite direction.

Dehydrated
A person becomes dehydrated when they lose a lot of water from their body. Food can also be dehydrated in order to preserve it and make it lighter to carry.

Desalinator
Equipment that is used by sailors for taking the salt out of sea water, making it possible to drink.

Dinghy
A small pleasure-boat or a small, rubber, inflatable boat attached to a ship and used in emergencies.

Distress beacon
This can be a fire or a light used as a signal to call for help. Nowadays, more sophisticated satellite distress beacons are usually used, which enable people to be located very accurately (see **GPS**).

Doldrums (the)
An area of sea just north of the Equator where the winds are extremely light. Boats often get stuck here for long periods of time.

Epic
Heroic or grand.

Equator
Imaginary line round the middle of the world at latitude 0°.

FAI
Stands for the organization Fédération Aéronautique Internationale, an international aeronautical organization which is the official body for overseeing all world aviation records.

Four-wheel drive vehicle
A motorized vehicle that has power going to all four wheels, rather than just two. Used for rough terrain.

Frostbite
A condition common in very cold climates, when body tissue becomes frozen and may completely die.

Gale
A very strong wind.

Generator
A machine that produces power.

GPS
Stands for Global Positioning System. The network of man-made satellites (see **Satellite**) round the Earth, that is used to navigate.

Heave to
A term used by sailors meaning to stop sailing.

Helium
A very light gas.

Hemisphere
The northern or southern half of the world. The two hemispheres are divided by the Equator (see **Equator**).

Horizon
The line at which the Earth's surface and the sky appear to meet.

Hull
The main part of a ship, including the bottom, sides and deck.

Hypothermia
A dangerous condition that happens when the body loses heat faster than it can produce it.

Hypoxia
A condition that happens when your body doesn't get enough oxygen and causes you to feel very ill.

Iceberg
A very large chunk of floating ice that has broken off a glacier or ice shelf.

Immersion heater
An electric device which is placed in a liquid to heat it.

Initiative
To 'use your initiative' means you are the person to take the first step in doing something or starting something off.

Intercom
A system of communication by radio or telephone, usually within a ship or aircraft.

Jet stream
Fast-moving and very high up winds which occur where the warm tropical air meets the cooler air north and south of the Tropics (see **Tropic of Cancer**, **Tropic of Capricorn**).

Keel
The lengthwise structure along the base of a yacht or ship. On some vessels, the keel extends down like a blade to increase stability.

Knot
A unit of speed used for ships, aircraft and winds. Equivalent to one nautical mile (see below) per hour.

Latitude (lines of)
Imaginary lines that are used to give distances north and south of the Equator.

Liner
A large, luxurious passenger ship.

Log
A detailed record that sailors keep of their voyages and pilots of their flights.

Longitude (lines of)
Imaginary lines that are used to give distances east and west of the prime meridian.

Mast
A long pole set up on a ship's keel (see above) to support its sails.

Merchant
A tradesman, especially one who sells goods in foreign countries.

Microlight
A small aircraft for one or two people, with a tiny engine.

Mine
A type of bomb placed on or just underneath the ground. It explodes when someone or something steps or drives on to it. When many mines are placed in one area it is called a mine field.

Mutiny
A rebellion against authority; usually describes soldiers or sailors rising up against their officers.

Native
A person who is born in or comes from a specific area.

Nautical mile
Used for measuring distances at sea; a nautical mile is equivalent to 1.852 km or 1.5 land miles.

Navigate
The word navigate originally comes from a Latin word meaning 'to sail'. To navigate now means to plan your way between points, in planes and other forms of transport as well as boats.

Paralysed
Unable to move.

Pirate
A robber at sea.

Plunder
To steal goods from.

Poles
The North and South Poles are the most northern and southern points of the Earth.

Press gang
In the past, the army and the navy did not have enough volunteers. Press gangs were groups of men whose job was to roam the streets forcing others to join up, often with violence.

Privateer
Like a pirate (see above), but they were usually unofficially sent by a government to attack ships from other countries carrying valuable objects.

Rebel
A person who resists authority and rules.

Rigging
The system of ropes or chains which support a ship's masts.

Satellite
An object that circles a bigger object, e.g. the Moon is the Earth's largest satellite. A satellite can be a planet or a man-made object. (See **GPS**.)

Scurvy
A disease caused by lack of vitamin C.

Self-steering (system)
A system on some boats which keep them on a set course.

Señor
Spanish word meaning Sir or Mr.

Silk Road (or Route)
Also known as the Spice Route, this is an ancient overland trade route linking central China with Europe.

Single-handed
When you do something single-handed, you do it alone, without help from anyone.

Snorkel
A tube for a swimmer to breathe through while underwater.

Sponsor
A person or organization that provides funds for a project or activity, usually in return for advertising.

Stagnant (water)
Having no current or flow.

Stamina
The ability to keep going physically and/or mentally.

Strait
A narrow passage of water connecting two large areas of water or seas.

Submerged
When something is underwater.

Swell
A slow, regular movement of the sea in rolling waves that do not break.

Tropic of Cancer
Imaginary line round the world 23° north of the Equator.

Tropic of Capricorn
Imaginary line round the world 23° south of the Equator.

Tropical
Describes the areas around the Tropics, i.e. hot and humid.

Tumour
A swelling of part of the body caused by an abnormal growth of tissue.

Turbulence
This is what can make a plane trip bumpy. It happens when the

air has been disturbed by gusty winds, changing temperature or other aircraft.

Typhoon
Hurricanes and cyclones are called typhoons in the north-west Pacific. They are tropical storms, usually about 400 miles (640 km) across, with strong winds and heavy rain.

Uninhabited
Not lived in or on.

Visa
A document which gives you permission to enter a foreign country. You have to apply to that country's government to get one.

Yacht
A sailing boat.

Yoga
A Hindu art involving meditation, breath control and bodily postures, to encourage health and relaxation.

FURTHER EXPLORATION

If you would like to find out more about any of the explorers, adventurers and expeditions that you have read about in this book, there are lots of things you can do. Look out for special exhibitions and talks and find out what's on at local museums. You can also find more books in the library and look up web sites on the Internet – often people who are making a round-the-world attempt have their own official website.

Places to visit:
Knox-Johnston's yacht *Suhaili* at The National Maritime Museum, Greenwich, London.
Chichester's yacht *Gipsy Moth IV* at *Cutty Sark* Gardens, Greenwich, London.
The National Museum of Science & Industry, Kensington, London.
Royal Airforce Museum, Hendon, London.
Ulster Folk & Transport Museum, Belfast.
Museum of Transport, Glasgow.
The Fleet Air Arm Museum, Yeovilton, Somerset.

Websites to visit:
National Maritime Museum - http://www.nmm.ac.uk
Pete Goss (round-the-world sailor) - http://www.petegoss.com

Some books you might enjoy reading:
Anderson, Dale, *Explorers Who Found New Worlds*, Steck-Vaughn, Texas, USA, 1994.
Arnold, Nick, *Voyages of Exploration*, Wayland, England, 1995.
Everett, Felicity and Reid, Struan, *The Usborne Book of Explorers*, London, 1991.
Explorer, Matthews, Rupert, Dorling Kindersley Eyewitness Guide, London, 1993.

The author would like to thank the following organizations for their assistance:
Royal Geographical Society, London.
Expedition Advisory Centre, RGS, London
National Maritime Museum, Greenwich, London.

Ulster Folk & Transport Museum, Northern Ireland.
Yachting World Magazine, London.
Guinness World Records, London.
Libraries in Belfast and County Down, Northern Ireland.

The author would also like to thank the many individuals who have helped her and, in particular, her editor, Amanda Li.

Bibliography

Anderson, Dale, *Explorers Who Found New Worlds*, Steck-Vaughn Company, USA, 1994.
Arnold, Nick, *Voyages of Exploration*, Wayland, England, 1995.
Bannister, Keith, *The Book of the Shark*, Grange Books, 1998
Bond, Bob, *The Handbook of Sailing*, Dorling Kindersley, London, 1994.
Bonnington, Chris, *Quest for Adventure*, Hodder & Stoughton, London, 1981.
British Antarctic Survey – various publications.
Bullimore, Tony, *Saved*, Little, Brown & Co, London, 1997.
Campbell, Ffyona, *The Whole Story*, Orion, London, 1996.
Chichester, Francis, *Gipsy Moth Circles the World*, World Books, London, 1968.
Curtis, Neil & Allaby, Michael, *Planet Earth*, Kingfisher Books, New York, 1993.
Davison, Ann, *My Ship is so Small,* Peter Davis, London, 1956.
The Dorling Kindersley Geography of the World, London, 1996.
Ellis, Richard, *The Book of Sharks*, Grosset & Dunlap, New York, 1976.
Everett, Felicity, & Reid, Struan, *The Usborne Book of Explorers*, Usborne, London, 1991.
Fiennes, Ranulph, *To the Ends of the Earth – Transglobe Expedition 1979–82*, Hodder & Stoughton, London, 1983.
First Aid Manual, Dorling Kindersley, London, 1988.
Foster, Lloyd, *Ostar*, Foulis, England, 1989.
James, Naomi, *Courage at Sea – Tales of Heroic Voyages*, Stanley Paul, London, 1987.
Goss, Pete, *Close to the Wind*, Headline, London, 1998
Graves, Richard, *Achievements – Land, Sea & Air: A Century of Conquest*, Blitz, Leicester, England, 1998
The Guinness Book of Records, Guinness Publishing Ltd, London, 1998 (and other years).
Hynson, Colin, *Magellan & The South Americas*, Ticktock Publishing Ltd, England, 1998.

Johnson, Peter, *The Encyclopedia of Yachting*, Dorling Kindersley, London, 1997.

Johnson, Peter, *The Guinness Book of Yachting Facts and Feats*, Guinness Superlatives Ltd, Middlesex, 1975.

Kunst, David, & Trowbridge, Clinton, *The Man Who Walked Around the World*, William Morrow, New York, 1979.

Matthews, Rupert, *Explorer*, Dorling Kindersley Eyewitness Guide, London, 1993.

Macquitty, Amanda, *Shark*, Dorling Kindersley Eyewitness Guide, London, 1992

The Oxford Children's Illustrated Encyclopedia, Oxford University Press, England, 1998.

Pennington, Piers, *The Great Explorers*, Bloomsbury Books, London, 1989.

People and the Sea, National Maritime Museum, London, (teacher's resource booklet)

Pigafetta, Antonio, *Magellan's Voyage, A Narrative Account of the First Circumnavigation*, Yale University Press, 1969.

Place, Francois, *The Discovery of the World – Navigators & Explorers*, Moonlight Publishing, London, 1989.

Rescue in the Southern Ocean, Penguin Books in association with The Age, Melbourne, Australia, 1997.

Slocum, Captain Joshua, *Sailing Alone Around the World*, Sheridan House, USA, 1995.

Varley, Carol, & Miles, Lisa, T*he Usborne Geography Encyclopedia*, London, 1997.

Verne, Jules, *Around the World in Eighty Days*, Everyman, 1994.

Walker, Jane, *Sharks*, Aladdin Books, London, 1993.

Watt, Fiona, *The Usborne Book of the Earth*, London, 1992

Wilson, Derek, *The Circumnavigators*, Constable and Company Ltd, London, 1989.

Yeager, Jeana, & Rutan, Dick, with Patton, Phil, *Voyager*, Heinemann, London, 1988.

Various magazines and newspapers including *Yachting World* and *GEOGRAPHICAL, THE MAGAZINE THAT EXPLORES THE WORLD.*

INDEX

Numbers in bold refer to illustrations.

006983

ACKNOWLEDGEMENTS

The author and publisher would like to thank the following for permission to include copyrighted quotations in this book:

Page 1 Quotation by Tony Bullimore from *Saved* by Tony Bullimore, published by Little Brown & Co, London.

Page 2 Quotation by Tony Bullimore from *Saved* by Tony Bullimore, published by Little Brown & Co, London; Quotation by Rob Penn, from GEOGRAPHICAL, THE MAGAZINE THAT EXPLORES THE WORLD; Quotation by David Kunst from *The Man Who Walked Around the World*, published by Morrow, USA, 1979, reproduced with permission of Sanford J Greenberger Associates.

Page 31 Quotation by Antonio Pigafetta, from *Magellan's Voyage, A Narrative Account of the First Circumnavigation* by Antonio Pigafetta, Yale University Press, 1969.

Page 45 Quotation by Francis Chichester from *Gipsy Moth Circles the World* by Francis Chichester. Reproduced with permission of Curtis Brown Ltd, London, on behalf of the Estate of Francis Chichester. Copyright Francis Chichester 1967.

Page 69 Quotations from *Rescue in the Southern Ocean*, Penguin Australia in association with The Age, Melbourne, Australia, 1997.

Page 116 Quotation by Ffyona Campbell from *The Whole Story* by Ffyona Campbell, published by Orion.

Page 129 Material by Rob Penn, precised from his article in *GEOGRAPHICAL*, THE MAGAZINE THAT EXPLORES THE WORLD.